MOUNI ABDELLI

WILD YEAST

The French Baker's Guide
to Making Your Own Starter
for Delicious Bread, Pizza,
Desserts, and More!

rockynook

Wild Yeast: The French Baker's Guide to Making Your Own Starter for Delicious Bread, Pizza, Desserts, and More!

Mouni Abdelli

Editor: Kelly Reed
Translation: Marie Deer
Copyeditor: Barbara Richter
Proofreader: Elizabeth Welch
Graphic design and layout: Anne Krawczyk
Layout and Cover Production: Randy Miyake
Project manager: Lisa Brazieal
Marketing coordinator: Mercedes Murray
All photographs and illustrations © Mouni Abdelli

ISBN: 978-1-68198-699-9
1st Edition (1st printing, December 2020)

Original French title: Faire son levain
© 2018 Éditions Eyrolles, Paris, France
French ISBN: 978-2-212-67504-7

Rocky Nook Inc.
1010 B Street, Suite 350
San Rafael, CA 94901
USA

www.rockynook.com

Distributed in the UK and Europe by Publishers Group UK
Distributed in the U.S. and all other territories by Ingram Publisher Services

Library of Congress Control Number: 2020941837

This book is printed on acid-free paper.
Printed in China

CONTENTS

INTRODUCTION

In this age where everything goes too fast, can we reclaim the pleasure we get from doing simple things that require a little more patience? In our frantic race toward greater productivity and less personal satisfaction, is it so crazy to hope that we could take a step back with respect to the most basic elements of our daily life, things like making our own bread?

I remember my mother and the ritual with which she made bread: the choice of ingredients; the kneading, which she often did by hand; the traditions, like not leaving the doors open to avoid the drafts that might have affected the rising of the dough. . . . As children, we never asked questions; we were too busy waiting for the bread to be baked so that we could savor it hot, just plain or covered with a thin film of good farm butter. There was something magical in that moment! A magic that we have forgotten over time, as rushed as we are!

What if, finally, the most important ingredient in making true good bread is simply time? I asked myself that question recently, after having spent some time pleasantly examining a batch of bread dough as though it were the most fascinating thing in the world. What is satisfying to me is rediscovering real bread, bread that takes time to make but is so worth it.

I also learned that this slow process could not only bring me a great deal of pride but could also be healthier. For a very long time, I thought it was a wonderful thing to be able to bake up a loaf of par-baked bread in less than 30 minutes. But over time, I began to enjoy it less and less and even found it harder and harder to digest, and I was far from being alone in that. . . .

If you think about it, bread, the idea of bread, is both extremely simple and very complex. Some flour, some water, some salt—these ordinary ingredients are enough to produce this "divine" food. So how can we help but be amazed by this process that has allowed the human race to benefit from wheat in so many ways, by this mixture that, once transformed, can give rise to an entirely different food, one that is fragrant, richly savory, and that stimulates every one of our senses?

Have you ever tried to chew a few grains of raw wheat? Not only is it very tough, but there isn't much to be gained from it. The transformation of the grains, however, allows us to develop a multitude of nutrients and flavors that continue to give us pleasure with every bite of bread that we take.

AN ANCIENT FOOD

For centuries, before instant baking yeast was developed and then marketed commercially, our ancestors produced nutritious breads using natural leavening. The development of a natural wild yeast, then, is simply a return to the origins of breadmaking.

At first, grains were eaten in the form of a mash, a little like porridge, and in Europe, it was usually made with rye. We would have a hard time recognizing the connection between that food and the bread that we eat today. The origins of the first bread made from wild yeast are hazy, but several sources attribute it to the Egyptians: someone supposedly, probably by accident, left a mixture of raw grains out somewhere that was exposed to the air and to wild yeast at ambient temperature, which gave it the opportunity to ferment and to swell. This process would have had to be followed by baking (someone had to think of that!), and that is supposedly how the ancestor of bread made from wild yeast was born!

Be that as it may, bread made from a natural starter is the result of a slow process that drew on wild yeast and bacteria, mainly lactobacilli. For more than five thousand years, bread was only produced through the synergy of these two microorganisms. Their combination allows bread to rise and gives it a lot of flavor, but it also allows the mixture's full nutritional potential to emerge. Baker's yeast, on the other hand, with its very quick acting time, has drastically reduced fermentation time, which is essential to the complex development of bread's aromas and digestibility.

THE BENEFITS OF BREAD MADE FROM WILD YEAST

The digestibility and the nutritiousness of bread that has been fermented through this process are very important points. The process of breadmaking using a natural wild yeast starter, which is a result of the action of lactic acid bacteria that break down sugars and thus produce lactic and acetic acids, lowers the pH of the dough and thus makes it more acidic. This acidification has a number of benefits. Grains contain phytic acid, which is present in large quantities in whole grains because it is mostly concentrated in the husk of the grain. But this phytic acid interferes with the proper assimilation of the minerals that are present in the grain. The acidification of the dough activates an enzyme called phytase, which allows the phytic acid to be broken down. This is why the slower preparation time is important: the more slowly the dough ferments, the more time the enzyme has to act and, therefore, to allow for the release and assimilation of all of this mineral potential. In addition, this acidification makes it possible for the bread to keep longer, unlike breads and other baked goods that are made quickly using baker's yeast, which tend to dry out as quickly as they are made.

Several writers have shown the advantage of eating bread made from wild yeast because of its lower glycemic index value and its greater digestive tolerability. It is assumed that the fermentation of the starter leads to a certain "predigestion" of the food because enzymatic processes, such as the action of protease (an enzyme that degrades gluten), act directly on the gluten and make it possible for it to be transformed. Thus, wild yeast may be well suited for people who suffer from intestinal discomfort connected with eating foods that contain gluten. The author Michael Pollan, who has become adept at making bread from wild yeast starter, explains in his culinary series *Cooked* (broadcast on Netflix, adapted from his best-selling book by the same name, Penguin Publishing Group, 2008) how the way we have been making "modern" bread for decades now has totally damaged our health. According to Pollan, methods of rapid bread-making, without any real fermentation and often based solely on white flours, have contributed to the development of food intolerances (especially of gluten) and metabolic disorders (such as diabetes) in more and more people. He is convinced that, for most of them, if they could just start eating bread that has been fermented slowly, they would soon forget the discomforts they had that were associated with the overconsumption of modern bread.

As for me, I have been making bread from wild yeast for several years now. At first, I went about it wrong: I was using the wild yeast starter more for the taste and the light acidity that it gave to the bread than for its health benefits. Not only that, but I was thinking of it like baker's yeast in the usual quantity and, thus, did not really allow the dough to rest. I thought I was making "wild yeast bread," but in fact, it was nothing more than slightly "improved" baker's yeast bread. Quite naturally, I ended up abandoning the procedure, telling myself that wild yeast was limiting and that I did not, ultimately, derive much benefit from it. How wrong I was!

A few years later, I discovered some photos of bread baked by Chad Robertson, a baker in San Francisco who was trained by Richard Bourdon, a guru of bread made from wild yeast, and also spent time with French bakers in Savoie and Provence. Robertson's popularity kept growing and growing—he is a true star among bakers and fans of wild yeast starter—and it was easy to see how well deserved that popularity was: you only had to see his bread to imagine tasting it! It has a beautiful caramelized crust and an airy cream-colored crumb, proof of the bread's authenticity and the baker's passion. This was nothing like the bread I had been making earlier. It was like a new challenge; I immediately decided to try the experience again!

Off I went to the natural foods store to stock up on flour, because I wanted to stack the odds in my favor. I figured some high-quality rye and wheat flour would be good to start with. A few utensils: a jar, a bowl, a rubber spatula, a pastry cutter, and the like—and I was ready! Armed with a recipe for a country bread from wild yeast starter, I threw myself back into this adventure, and I haven't stopped since. I have no regrets. All of my eating habits around bread and baked goods have changed. And my family and friends have rediscovered the taste of "real" bread. We digest it better, we feel fuller, and the sensory experience is better.

Good bread needs time, the time required for effective fermentation, which allows us to benefit from the nutrients that the grains have to offer; even if this process means that the dough has to rest for 8 to 12 hours, we have everything to gain!

This book is not intended to demonize commercial baker's yeast, which can certainly be added to certain recipes. My intention is mainly just to make it clear that a long, slow fermentation process is essential, as much for its health benefits as for the taste of the bread.

I baked all of the recipes in this book myself, using French flour, in the household oven of my tiny kitchen in the Paris region. So, there is no reason why you shouldn't be able to get the same results. Take the time to read each recipe carefully through, and most of all, have faith in yourself! Happy baking to you, my friends!

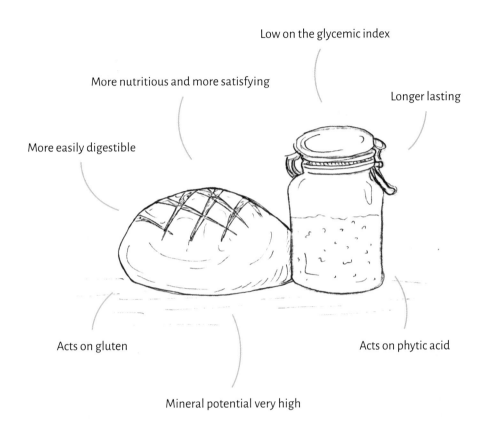

Low on the glycemic index

More nutritious and more satisfying

Longer lasting

More easily digestible

Acts on gluten

Acts on phytic acid

Mineral potential very high

1

BREADMAKING

Breadmaking requires three key ingredients: flour, water, and salt. Each of these plays a crucial role, but flour is still the most important component because it affects the final product's characteristics, such as volume, the appearance of the crumb, the crust, and the taste.

FLOUR

Breadmaking relies primarily on one precious ingredient, namely flour, and therefore, most often, on wheat, of which there are different varieties. Generally, a grain is said to be a bread-quality grain if it contains gluten. The main bread-quality grains, aside from hard wheat, are soft wheat, spelt, and rye. Hard-wheat flour, which is the flour most often used for making bread, is made up primarily of carbohydrates (starches and others), proteins (gluten), fat, water, vitamins, minerals, and enzymes.

On their way from the mill to our plates, the wheat grains undergo several different procedures in order to produce the flour that we know and eat. Bread-quality wheat has positive properties and positive capacities: it can be hydrated, the dough can be kneaded and fermented, and so on.

Wheat flour, once it has been hydrated, forms a mesh network that can trap the gases that result during fermentation. This network is a result of the composition of the flour, more specifically, of the two insoluble proteins that it contains: gliadin and, in smaller quantities, glutenin. These two proteins enter into the composition of gluten. Gliadin gives the dough the ability to stretch, whereas glutenin gives it elasticity and resilience (the ability to resist the stretching). These properties are related to the information about the flour's baking strength that is sometimes detailed on the packaging. Thus, the more gluten the flour contains, the more elastic and stretchable it will be, which influences its gas retention properties, which in turn affect the volume of the bread and the structure of the crumb.

TESTING THE FLOUR

It is important to remember that different kinds of flour, depending on their brand (even if they are of the same "T type"), contain different proportions of protein. The capacity to absorb liquid varies from one kind of flour to another and thus will involve modifications in recipes. Every kind of flour is unique and has its own specific absorption capacity. When you want to get started and you are not sure about the characteristics of the product you are using, start by slightly reducing the amount of water you use and then get used to handling the dough that you make with this flour, observing it and touching it. This is still the very best way to learn about it.

During the milling process, the bran and the germ of the wheat are mostly removed; the more thoroughly that is done, the lighter the appearance of the flour. White flour is made up mainly of the kernel of the wheat grain and part of the germ. The germ, which is rich in fat, speeds up the rancidification of the flour; this is particularly the case for stone-ground flours, in which the germ is retained.

Sometimes, the ash content of the flour will be indicated on the packaging, which corresponds to the amount of mineral content retained in the flour. This number, determined by the calcination of a flour sample, is strictly regulated. In France, for example, wheat flours are classified according to their ash content.

Throughout the book I refer to French flour designations along with the closest American equivalent flours. See below for a chart comparing both for easy reference:

French	Approximate American Equivalent
Type 45	Cake & Pastry
Type 55	All-Purpose
Type 65	High Gluten
Type 80	Light Whole Wheat
Type 110	Whole Wheat
Type 150	Dark Whole Wheat

In addition to wheat flour, other kinds of flour can also be used, most often in combination with wheat to compensate for their lack of gluten; one of these is rye flour, which I use regularly, both for making bread and for maintaining my starter. If you want to choose two main kinds of flour for your start on the wild yeast adventure, I recommend those two.

Rye flour is also available in various varieties: light, medium, and dark. It is rich in minerals, and while it is poor in gluten, it has a high absorption capacity. Grayish in color, it has a characteristically malty flavor. I usually buy it in organic grocery stores or directly from flour mills.

In this book, you will find recipes featuring a variety of kinds of flour, such as spelt flour, which is rich in fat and minerals and is another good bread-quality flour with a slightly nutty taste you will enjoy; Kamut® flour, which is produced from Khorasan wheat, grown exclusively in organic agriculture, and is higher in protein than soft wheat; and many more. The idea here is to encourage you to test new combinations by playing with the texture, appearance, and aroma of the bread.

PROPER STORAGE OF FLOUR

It is important to keep your flour in a cool, dry spot. This is even more the case for so-called milled flours, which are high in germ content and therefore more fragile.

Do not give in to the temptation to buy 25-kilogram bags of flour, which are meant for professionals. Those quantities are packaged to meet the needs of professional bakers, while a dedicated hobby baker, using smaller amounts, is going to have to store what is left over and will eventually notice that, as the weeks and months go by, the dough behaves differently because the flour has deteriorated over time. Thus, it is a better choice to buy your flour in small packages or, if you are making bread every day, in 5- to 10-kilogram bags at the most. This will avoid waste and unpleasant surprises!

WHAT ABOUT
HOMEMADE FLOUR?

Making flour involves a lot of know-how, and you can't just make yourself into an instant miller. But many of us are interested in trying to make our own flour at home anyhow, something that many amateur bakers enjoy doing, especially in the United States.

It is indeed a real pleasure to work with fresh, "living" flour, and it provides many benefits, starting with nutrition, because you can grind your flour as you go along, thus retaining all of the potential of the grain. This procedure also provides an advantage in taste, because fresh flour is much more flavorful. And while freshly ground flour is more fragile, it also has the benefit of being produced only as needed, which eliminates the need for long-term storage.

People have tried a variety of ways to produce flour at home inexpensively, for instance by using a coffee grinder. The results are unreliable, however, and the machine has a tendency to break after a few uses. So if you really want to begin and invest yourself in this process, you will need to equip yourself with a grain mill that is worthy of the name!

Several different home models are available online, but the price is nevertheless still often prohibitive, in particular for occasional use, and most of the models are also quite bulky. In addition, if you want to use anything aside from whole-grain flour, you will have to buy specific sieves for each different kind of flour, allowing you to produce white, whole-grain, or "bise" (light whole-grain) flour. Certain brands, including the Moulins d'Alma, offer sets of three sieves in varying sizes, allowing you to produce these three different kinds of flour.

Some models can be attached to food processors (such a KitchenAid); the one I have chosen for myself is a Mockmill (see photo on page 26), which combines efficiency with a smaller size. In a small Parisian kitchen, that is a big advantage!

To make your homemade flour, you will, of course, also need some grain: wheat, rye, einkorn wheat, spelt, and the like. These are not always easy to find anywhere but in natural food stores. However, if you are able to buy them directly from a grain producer or a mill, you will start out with better information about the source, characteristics, and best use of the grains you plan to grind.

WATER

Water should be considered as an ingredient in its own right. We tend to underestimate its importance, but it plays a key role in breadmaking.

To begin with, water is essential for hydrating the flour: when the water and flour are mixed together, they will start to form a dough, thanks to the hydration of the starch and the gluten. Water also plays a role in activating the enzymatic and fermentation processes. And finally, it serves to dissolve other ingredients, such as salt. It is important to note that the quantity of water, which is to say the degree of hydration of the dough, will affect fermentation: the more hydrated the dough, the faster the fermentation (and, conversely, the less hydrated the dough, the slower the fermentation).

The quantity of water also plays a role in the texture and consistency of the dough, even apart from the absorption qualities of the flour. If you use too much water, the dough will be too sticky and hard to work with. The quantity of water can be expressed by a hydration rate that corresponds to the proportion of water in the dough, and it is often expressed in relation to 1 kilogram of flour. A dough that uses 1000 grams of flour and has a total of 650 grams of water, therefore, has a hydration rate of 65%.

Do not add the amount of water specified in the recipe all at once if you are not accustomed to the flour you are using or if you have not mastered the handling of soft dough. You have to find a happy medium, and as with the flour, you need to gradually experiment to determine the right amount of water, depending on the consistency you will be most comfortable working with. This is especially true if you are trying out a foreign recipe. American flours, in particular, do not have the same qualities or absorption capacities as French flours. It is essential to start by reducing the amount of water from what is given in the recipe and then to add more, progressively, depending on how the dough behaves as you are kneading it. This will help you to avoid ending up with a large, sticky, almost liquid mass that is impossible to shape.

The temperature of the water also affects fermentation. The room temperature during the preparation of the dough, the temperature of the ingredients, and the kneading will all determine the final temperature of the dough. You can also play with the fermentation using the water temperature. In the summer, for instance, it's a good idea to use cooler water, and even to put the flour in the refrigerator, to avoid having the fermentation speeded up too much by the higher room temperature. In the winter, on the other hand, you can use warmer water to compensate for the lower room temperature so that the fermentation will not be slowed down.

The composition of the water also affects fermentation; I use filtered water (for instance, using a Brita filter) to make my bread and maintain my starter; I suggest that you do the same. The water that we normally drink has undergone several different kinds of treatment that could have a negative effect on the dough, especially the chlorine treatment, which leaves chlorine residues in the water that could cause problems because of their disinfectant action. By filtering the water, you can minimize these effects. If you don't have a water filter, you can also simply fill a bottle with tap water and let it stand for a few hours before using it, which will help to lower the amount of chlorine, for instance, in the water.

And finally, the steam that is released during baking allows the bread to develop properly and to produce a lovely, delicate, golden crust!

SALT

While we use salt every day to enhance the taste of what we cook, salt also plays an important role in breadmaking, not just for its ability to bring out flavor but also for its function in the breadmaking process. This is true at every stage of the process, including during the baking itself.

Beginning with the first phase of preparation, the salt comes into contact with the proteins in the flour. This interaction gives stability to the glutinous network, which will later allow for better retention of the fermentation gases, whose speed will be slowed down and regulated by the presence of salt.

In addition, salt has hygroscopic properties, which means that it retains water and humidity. (This is why you are advised never to let baker's yeast come into contact with salt, which would tend to dehydrate it.) But these properties also make the dough easier to work with and make it possible to slow down the drying out of the final product. They also guarantee a lovely, delicate, golden crust during baking.

There are various kinds of salt that are commercially available. I most often use untreated, unrefined sea salt in my bread recipes.

TEMPERATURE

I consider temperature to be an essential parameter for the success of bread made from wild yeast starter; the room temperature and the temperature of the ingredients will greatly influence the process.

Bacteria react differently depending on the heat: a low temperature will favor the development of acetic acidity, whereas a higher temperature will allow for a so-called lactic acidity, which is milder.

A good temperature for the starter is around 81 to 86°F (27 to 30°C). Even though heat increases bacterial activity, excessively high temperatures will compromise the fermentation, just as excessively low temperatures will make the dough taste too acidic.

In addition to its impact on the starter, the temperature affects the fermentation of the bread dough, especially if you look at the temperature of the dough when you have finished kneading. At this stage, the temperature will generally be about 73 to 77°F (23 to 25°C). Some technical publications and professional recipe cards refer to the base temperature. This is calculated using the room temperature and the temperature of the water and of the flour. Even though, as home cooks, we would rarely have that information, it does seem logical to take into account the temperature of the ingredients, especially of the water and the flour. As we saw earlier, it is easy enough to store your flour in a cool place when it is too hot out or to adjust the temperature of the water, both of which are simple things you can do to carry out your fermentation under favorable conditions.

INGREDIENTS AND COLORS

You can incorporate a variety of ingredients into your dough to add color. You can choose spices like turmeric, which will produce a flamboyantly colored bread, or even charcoal powder, which will give you a black bread that won't go unnoticed!

The best thing is to use natural dyes. It would be a shame to go straight for chemical dyes when nature offers us such a vast array of choice! There are powders, purees, liquids, and various tricks for coloring bread dough naturally. At the same time, though, you should beware of certain products that might potentially also add flavor, whereas others are so discreet that you will never notice their taste and only their color will show up!

Here are some examples of coloring agents you can use to get the following colors:

- Green: spinach (chlorophyll), matcha tea, spirulina, pistachio paste
- Yellow: turmeric, curry
- Orange: carrot, pumpkin
- Red: paprika, tomato, beet
- Purplish pink: red cabbage, red fruits (blueberries), purple carrots, hibiscus
- Black: powdered activated carbon, cuttlefish ink
- Brown beige: malt, cacao
- Blue: petals of blue pea (Clitoria ternatea) to be infused in water

It is fairly simple to incorporate these ingredients into the dough when they are in liquid form, like carrot juice; all you have to do is replace some or all of the liquid in the recipe with the juice. The same is true for purees. For spices and powders, however, you have to just gradually add them until you get the color you want. I usually add between a teaspoon and a tablespoon for 500 grams of flour.

For a very dramatic effect, only color part of the dough: this will allow you to make bread loaves that alternate between colored and neutral zones, which is guaranteed to give you unusual and psychedelic effects.

Orange yellow bread with turmeric

Brioches with pistachio paste

Black bread with activated charcoal

Colorful bread with red cabbage

2

UTENSILS

There is no need to go broke buying materials to make good bread from wild yeast. Most of the utensils used in the recipes here are basic ones. Aside from the little bit of equipment you will need for mixing the batter, shaping it, or handling the dough, you will need a few spoons and spatulas, parchment paper, and gloves. In this chapter, you will find a listing of the utensils I use regularly, along with their benefits and a few alternatives.

ELECTRIC SCALE

This may seem obvious: a kitchen scale is essential. You can make bread, even great bread, by relying only on the texture of your batter, but that is often a challenge for a beginner. Using a scale is even more important when you are starting and maintaining a wild yeast starter culture. The recipes in this book are based on a starter that has been hydrated to 100%, which means that it contains the same quantity of water as it does of flour. Because you will need to adhere to this ratio for the recipe to succeed properly, the recipes in this book list the ratios for all ingredients, including the liquid ingredients, in grams. Always begin by weighing all of the ingredients, because even though you can use spoon measurements for some optional fillings, it is important to weigh the main ingredients of the recipe, which are flour, water, salt, and the wild yeast starter.

JARS

To start and maintain a wild yeast starter, you will need at least one jar with a lid, ideally one made out of glass. Failing that, a plastic jar with a lid will work too. I recommend that you only use transparent containers, which will allow you to observe the starter and to monitor its activity more easily. Also note that while you will be able to use small containers like jam jars when you are first establishing a starter, as the days go by it will be harder to make do with those, because the starter may well start to overflow.

BOWLS

When it's time to refresh, or "feed," the starter, a small bowl will allow you to mix the ingredients directly and ensure that the mixture is well aerated before you transfer it into a jar. When you are preparing the bread dough itself and combining all of the ingredients, you will have to use a large bowl.

Although some people prefer to mix their ingredients right on their work surface, I personally do not find that very practical, especially when the dough is very sticky or the work surface small. You can use the food processor bowl; otherwise, a large salad bowl will do the job. Some containers even come with their own fitted lid, which is very convenient and means that you will not have to use plastic wrap.

DOUGH MIXER

Using an electric dough mixer can save you an enormous amount of time and energy, but when you are just starting, I strongly recommend that you knead the dough by hand in order to feel it and become familiar with it. Different kinds of flour and different levels of hydration will result in different textures for your dough, and the best way to judge that is to touch the dough, stretch it, and fold it. You do all of these things with your fingers, and no utensil is more sensitive or efficient than your own hands. You will find a simple kneading method on page 51 is just the first page of the chapter, not the kneading method. Just giving the chapter should be enough. "Dough: The Key Steps."

Once you have familiarized yourself with the texture and appearance of the dough that you want to make, it will be easier in the future to knead the dough using an electric dough mixer, which is, in fact, an extraordinary tool, especially for very wet and sticky dough.

The recipes in this book can be made using only the dough mixer (for myself, I use a KitchenAid with a hook attachment). I don't give any specific kneading times because I think that is too abstract for a home baker. I believe that it is more appropriate to learn to observe the dough throughout the process of kneading, especially when the dough has been prepared by hand ahead of time.

Safety
During the kneading, you will often have to stop the machine in order to scrape the edges of the bowl so that the ingredients can fall back into the center and the hook can reach them all. Watch out for your fingers; never do this while the machine is running!

AIRTIGHT JARS OR BOXES

A plastic or glass storage box with an airtight lid can replace the bowl during the fermentation stage. This is very convenient when you need to allow the dough to rest in a cool place for a few hours; it takes up less space and will make it easy for you to make folds in the dough (see chapter 4) while monitoring the dough's increase in volume.

BANNETONS
(PROOFING BASKETS)

Banneton, or proofing basket, is what we call the basket used in the last phase of fermentation, the proofing (see chapter 4), right before the bread is baked. Originally made out of wicker, they can also be found in plastic, in different shapes and sizes. Some of them are covered with linen fabric to make it easier to remove the dough.

These baskets are handy for maintaining the shape of the dough, but if you don't have one, a small basket or a bowl covered with a floured dishcloth will work as well. Ideally, the banneton should be floured with rice flour, which makes things a lot easier and avoids unpleasant surprises when you unmold the dough before baking, especially for a high hydration dough.

BAKER'S COUCHE

Some kinds of bread, like baguettes, are set out to ferment during the proofing stage on floured linen baker's couche cloth. It is a good idea to brush it regularly. You can also use thick, floured dishcloths.

BAKING DISHES

After trying out several different ways of baking my bread at home in my kitchen oven, I quickly realized that the best way to achieve uniform baking with a good amount of steam was to use a baking dish (such as a Dutch oven, a bread cloche, or a casserole dish). The advantage is that you don't have to worry about the steam, and you can put the bread straight into the oven (after having made sure to preheat the baking dish and its lid).

There are various kinds of baking dishes, including the legendary Le Creuset. For bread cloches, there is a much narrower range of choices. The only real drawback of using a baking dish is that the bread has to be shaped in such a way that it can be baked in it. For more unusual shapes, you will have to use a different baking method, such as a baking stone.

BAKING STONE OR PIZZA STONE

A baking stone, or pizza stone, is an excellent basis for baking breads like baguette, ciabatta, and, of course, pizza at home. These stones are available in a variety of sizes, shapes, and thicknesses, and sometimes come with peels that allow you to easily transfer the dough to the stone. You will need to make sure, before you buy one, that the size of the stone matches the width of your oven, especially for rectangular models. Note that the stone must be preheated at the same time as the oven, usually about 45 to 60 minutes before you start baking the bread. To make it easier, turn the loaf directly out of the baking dish onto parchment paper and then slide it onto the stone using the peel or a plate or tray.

PASTRY CUTTER OR DOUGH SCRAPER

A dough cutter is an essential tool for making bread, and even more so when you are working with a dough that is a little bit sticky. I use the dough cutter to detail the dough, to pre-shape it, to transfer the dough into the baking dish, and to scrape and clean my work surface. It's really very handy! But if you don't have one, a good knife will allow you to cut the dough just as easily.

A rigid dough scraper (a plastic half-moon-shaped scraper) is also very useful for scraping the sides of the bowl, especially during kneading. You can also use it with some doughs that are highly hydrated for making folds. If you don't have a dough scraper, a large silicone spatula can also work.

BREAD SCORER OR BLADE

A bread scorer, which looks a lot like a scalpel, allows you to make incisions and to easily score your loaf before putting it in the oven. There are several different models of scorers, from the most basic to the most sophisticated. You can even use a razor blade mounted on a wooden handle or a very sharp small knife. Always remember to protect the blade when you put it away!

SPRAY BOTTLE
OR LAVA ROCKS

Unlike what can be done in a professional baker's oven, you can't inject steam into a regular kitchen oven. However, there are a few different things you can do to create a favorable environment for your baking. For example, a little spray bottle filled with water is perfect for breads baked on a baking stone, although there is the issue that you have to open the hot oven to spray.

Another method is to use lava rocks, which are readily available from online stores or stores selling barbecue equipment. Just put a few of them into a dish that you put in the oven, preheating them at the same time as the baking stone, and pour boiling water over them when you put the bread in the oven. They will then release steam, and you will not have to open the oven again in the first few minutes of baking.

If you use a baking dish, this is not something you have to worry about.

3

WILD YEAST STARTER, A USER'S GUIDE

Now it is time to learn how to make your own starter. We will look at how to start it, maintain it day after day, and, especially, how to use it to make superb bread!

FLOUR
AND WATER

Making your own wild yeast starter and maintaining it is very simple; you just have to follow a few rules and, above all, be observant.

When you are embarking on the adventure of wild yeast and have not yet mastered it, you may run into some frustrations, especially if your first attempts are not convincing, or if you had a bad experience years ago that you are still carrying around with you. Don't forget that your starter is alive and that there will be times when it is extremely active and other times when you will find it to be a little more sluggish. The secret to making your adventure a success lies in the care and patience that you bring to it. If the week's worth of time that you need for establishing a wild yeast starter feels burdensome to you, remember that that is what will then allow you to have a starter that can last for years, if you maintain it properly. And in fact, that is also the magic of wild yeast: the idea that a culture can last a very, very long time and that it will be almost unique every time! Your first attempts might seem fruitless, but with a little bit of perseverance, you will see results.

It all starts with the development of a spontaneous culture, which, given a favorable environment, will live on and be able to produce dough forever. There are different ways to make a wild yeast starter, but the basic idea is almost always the same—to start a culture using water and flour, to feed it by giving it another mixture of water and flour every time, to eliminate part of it, and so on. . . .

To start a spontaneous culture, I will make a mixture of (for example) a particular quantity of T65 (high-gluten) wheat flour and the same quantity of rye flour (let's say 250 grams of each). I then store this mixture in an airtight container and use it regularly, beginning from when I establish the starter and again every time I feed it.

Worth Knowing
The wild yeast starter that is made and used in all of the recipes in this book is a liquid starter at 100% hydration. This means that the starter is always established and renewed using an equal mixture of flour and water. This produces a semi-liquid starter, like a pancake batter.

A MATTER OF HYDRATION

In addition to liquid starter, there is a so-called hard, or firm, starter, whose hydration rate is often close to 50%, which means that the quantity of water is half that of the flour.

The choice between the two is, first and foremost, a question of taste. Personally, I am a fan of a young, liquid starter that has fruity notes and is not very aggressive when it is properly maintained. A liquid starter will tend to develop lactic flavors, whereas a firm starter will more likely have strong aromas and acetic notes.

The starter's degree of hydration will also be reflected in the texture of the dough, affecting its strength and stretchiness. Having tried both kinds, I now only use liquid starters for everything I make, whether it's a recipe for baguettes or for croissants.

However, if you want to use a firm starter, at 50% hydration, that is easy enough to manage just by converting your liquid starter. All you have to do is refresh it using a given quantity of flour and half that quantity of water. For example, if you have 50 grams of 100% liquid starter, you can refresh it with 50 grams of flour but only 25 grams of water.

PREPARING YOUR LIQUID WILD YEAST STARTER

Ingredients and Basic Materials

Mixture of equal parts of T65 (high-gluten) wheat flour and of whole-wheat flour

Water (preferably filtered)

Small bowl

Jar with lid

Wooden spoon or small spatula

Day 1: Pour 50 grams of the flour mixture and 50 grams of water into a small bowl. Mix well, using the wooden spoon, to homogenize and aerate the preparation.

Worth Knowing

The preparation of the initial mixture and of the refreshments (the mixtures that one adds to the wild yeast starter later to feed it) takes place in a bowl, before being transferred to the jar. This allows you to thoroughly homogenize the starter and to avoid letting part of it stay in the bottom of the container without being properly incorporated.

Transfer the 100 grams of preparation to the jar, which has been rinsed with hot water ahead of time, and let it ferment in a warm location until the next day (for 24 hours).

Day 2: Depending on the room temperature and the kind of flour you are using, it might already be possible to observe the first signs of fermentation. This is highly variable, however, and you should absolutely not be discouraged if you do not see any; it is still much too early to judge.

Now it is time to feed the wild yeast starter for the first time. For this refreshment of the starter, and for the entire time that you are getting your starter established, it will be necessary to discard part of it every time. Don't worry, this will not last forever, and once the starter is established, you won't have to "waste" part of it anymore.

Of the previous day's mixture, which weighs 100 grams, keep only 50. Because this starter is hydrated at 100%, you need to keep feeding it the same quantity of water and flour (50 grams of the previous day's starter + 50 grams of flour + 50 grams of water). Here, again, it is very convenient to use premixed flour. Mix everything in the small bowl to aerate it, and then transfer it to the jar before letting it ferment again for 24 hours.

Days 3 to 5: For these three days, follow the same process as on day 2. Every day, keep only 50 grams of the previous day's mixture, and add 50 grams of water and 50 grams of mixed flour to that, with a rest of 24 hours between each feeding.

Days 6 to 8: Starting on day 6, the feedings take place two times a day, with a 12-hour interval between them. The procedure to be followed is the same as on the previous days, but with twice as many feedings, keeping only part of the starter (50 grams) each time.

If everything has gone well, at the end of these last three days, the starter will be ready to use; it will be very active and eager to get to work!

Our method is spread out over an average of 8 to 10 days so that the starter will be sufficiently active and ready to use. The time can be longer, but never shorter. A wild yeast starter is not considered to be stable from a microbiological standpoint until about 10 days have gone by.

CHECKING THAT THE WILD
YEAST STARTER IS READY

A simple little trick for checking that the starter is active enough to start a bread dough with is to give it the flotation test. All you have to do is to take a small quantity of the starter, a tablespoon for example, and pour it into a glass of water. If the starter is active enough, it should float and stay on the surface!

Worth Knowing

As I explained above, the 8-day time period is variable; the room temperature, the quantity of flour, and many other factors will affect the activity of the starter. You will need to keep observing and not become impatient. It is better to keep feeding and refreshing the starter for a few days longer so that it will be good and active than to hurry things and be disappointed, when all that the starter needed was a little more care! On the other hand, if there is still nothing happening after about 10 days, that is a bad sign. Try to determine what it was that got in the way of the proper development of the starter before starting over.

Establishing Your Starter

Day 1

50 grams
of water

50 grams
of flour
(rye + wheat)

Let stand
24 hours

Dispose of 50 grams of
the previous day's starter

Day 2

50 grams of the previous
day's starter

50 grams of flour

50 grams of water

Let stand
24 hours

Dispose of 50 grams of the
previous day's starter

Days 3 – 4 – 5

50 grams of the
previous day's starter

50 grams of flour

50 grams of water

1 feeding per day

Keep only 50 grams of the
previous day's starter

Let stand 24 hours
between each
feeding

Days 6 – 7 – 8

2 feedings per day
every 12 hours

Keep only 50 grams of the
previous preparation each time

50 grams of the previous
preparation

50 grams of flour

50 grams of water

Let stand 24 hours
after the final
feeding

IT'S READY!

FRUIT YEAST

The fascinating thing about wild yeast is that you can experiment forever. It never gets boring! Making wild yeast from fruit is nothing new, but the fun thing is experimenting and seeing that you can start yeast for breadmaking from almost any fruit or vegetable.

The best-known and most common way to make fruit yeast is to start with apples and raisins. The technique is very simple, and I recommend it if you are having trouble starting a "classic" wild yeast starter or if you are having trouble finding rye flour.

The procedure is simple and can be broken down into a few steps. Again, it might seem a little onerous, but most of the time, you just have to let nature take its course.

Ingredients and Basic Materials

Organic fruit: 2 apples and 1 handful of raisins

Water (preferably filtered)

Your choice of flour (whole-grain, rye, . . .)

Jar with a lid or bottle with a stopper (to be washed between each step)

Small bowl

Wooden spoon or small spatula

---

1. Prepare the fermentation of the fruit in water

Boil the jar or bottle and allow it to cool completely. Meanwhile, rinse the apples and quarter them.

Place the apples and the raisins in the container and cover them with filtered water (about 500 to 600 grams of water for 2 to 3 apples). Close the container and let it stand at room temperature for 3 to 5 days.

During this time, you will need to aerate the preparation twice a day. Afterward, reseal the container and shake it for a few seconds.

The fermented water is ready when it is fizzy, a little like a soft drink. As long as it is not fizzing and shows no signs of fermentation, there is no point in using it, because the fermentation is not complete.

2. Collect the fermented water

Once the fermented water has started fizzing and is ready to be used, filter it and discard the fruit.

Pour the water into a clean jar. Keep 50 grams of it at room temperature and reserve the rest, storing it in the refrigerator.

3. Establish a wild yeast starter from the fermented water

Into a bowl, pour the 50 grams of room-temperature fermented water and 50 grams of your choice of flour (either a wheat-rye mixture or whole-grain flour). Mix well with the wooden spoon to aerate the preparation. Then transfer the mixture into a clean jar that was previously rinsed with hot water.

Let it stand overnight at room temperature. With this process, the first signs of fermentation in the starter will appear fairly quickly.

4. Feed the fruit starter

Take the 100 grams of starter that was sitting out overnight—do not discard any of it—add 50 grams of the chilled fermented water, and then add 50 more grams of flour. Mix well to aerate and homogenize the preparation, return it to the jar, and cover it. Then let it ferment again for 6 to 12 hours depending on the room temperature.

After this rest, the 200 grams of starter should be showing definite signs of fermentation and bubbling generously. Now add 150 more grams of fermented fruit water and 150 more grams of flour. Mix well and let it stand at room temperature again for several hours, ideally observing the starter to judge the time necessary. On average, it will be ready to use after 4 hours.

This will give you 500 grams of fruit starter, which you can use right away to make bread according to whichever recipe you choose. You can also reduce the initial feeding quantities if you want to prepare only a small amount of fruit starter.

Personally, I prefer to use this freshly prepared fruit starter right away in a recipe, but if you want to maintain it, you can keep on maintaining it with flour and water in the same way as detailed above for classic wild yeast starter (see page 37).

WHAT ABOUT USING OTHER KINDS OF FRUIT?

You can try out several different combinations of fruits or vegetables to make your own unique fruit yeasts. The main principle is always the same: let it ferment for several days in water, filter it, and then use it to establish a starter to make bread with. Certain kinds of fruit or vegetables will give special flavors to the bread. My favorite is wild yeast starter made from lemon water, which is a treat!

DAILY MAINTENANCE OF YOUR WILD YEAST STARTER

Once the wild yeast starter has been established, and depending on how often you are going to use it, you will need to store it and maintain it so that you can use it for as long as possible.

For hobbyists who bake every day, the starter can be stored at room temperature and fed daily, once a day or, if it is very hot, twice a day. This process can be a little burdensome, but it has the advantage of strengthening the starter. Most of us, however, are more likely to use the starter a little less often, which is why we need to keep it in the refrigerator. In this way, it can be kept alive for several weeks, becoming partially dormant.

If I am going to be baking on the weekend, or only occasionally, I store my starter in a cool place after its last feeding and before it has reached a peak of activity. I then take out a small amount, depending on how much I need, which I feed a few hours before or the night before I make my bread dough. Now that I am well acquainted with my starter, I know that it can be ready in 4 to 5 hours, especially if it is hot enough in my kitchen. But because every starter is unique, some will need more like 6 to 8 hours to become active enough. Taking the time to observe your starter will also allow you to know how to use it best.

During my first attempts, I kept some of my starters in the refrigerator for a very long time, took them out when I needed them, and let them return to room temperature before feeding them. The disadvantage of that approach was that I had to discard some of the starter when I put it back into the refrigerator so that it would not become too acidic. During cold storage, the lactobacilli always remain a little bit active and the culture becomes more and more acidic. When the starter is refreshed, they wake up and are reactivated. If the starter has been kept cool for a very long time, it will definitely need to be fed at least two times to be reactivated correctly and so that you can obtain a soft, fruity starter.

Beyond the need to maintain the starter so that you will be able to make bread regularly, it is essential to feed it to maintain the flora in it so that the culture will not become completely lost or go moldy. When you store a starter in the refrigerator for several weeks, you have to feed it to maintain it, about every 7 to 10 days.

In practice, once the starter has been established and stored, if the recipe calls for 100 grams of active starter, I take out a small amount, about 20 grams, to which I add equal quantities of flour and water, in the proportions 20 grams of starter + 40 grams of flour (20 grams of wheat flour + 20 grams of rye flour) + 40 grams of water. I mix everything in a small bowl and pour it into a jar. You can use a marker to draw a line on the jar to mark the level of the starter; it will usually have tripled in volume by the time it reaches its peak.

These proportions are just an example; other people might prefer to use equal quantities of starter, flour, and water. This is a routine that you will gradually establish for yourself as you try it out; there are as many ways of doing it as there are starters, and every one is unique!

LONG-TERM STORAGE: DRIED WILD YEAST STARTER

There are several ways to preserve your starter—for instance, if you are going on vacation, if you have a surplus of active starter, or if you just want to have a little bit set aside just in case.

Some people prefer to freeze their starter, and others like to dry it by adding flour to make little patties. In my opinion, the most convenient and effective method, and more important, the one that allows you to maintain your starter the best, is to dehydrate it. It's easy, it hardly takes any room, and it works very well. It is also a good way to share it without damaging it.

DEHYDRATION

Ideally, the starter should be at least a few weeks old before it can be dehydrated. At that point, it will be robust enough to withstand this stress very well. The starter should also be very active, which means it needs to have been fed a few hours before the dehydration so that it will be at its peak during the dehydration operation.

To dehydrate the starter, take out the amount of active starter that you wish to preserve and, using a spatula, spread it in a thin layer on a sheet of parchment paper. The thinner the layer, the faster it will dry. Depending on the ambient conditions and the thickness of the layer of starter, the drying can take anywhere from a few hours to a few days.

Once the layer of starter has dried, the baking sheet will start to warp. At that point, it is necessary to detach the film of starter so that it will break and crumble into flakes, which can then be stored in a small jar with a lid or in a food storage bag. You can also use a mortar, for example, to crush them to a powder, or crush them with a rolling pin after sealing them in an airtight bag.

Once the starter has been turned into flakes or powder, it will keep very well in a dry place, protected from humidity, ideally at the back of a cool cupboard or a drawer.

REHYDRATION

To rehydrate a starter and restart it, take the amount you need—for example, 10 grams—and moisten it with the same quantity of water. Then add equal quantities of water and flour to keep a hydration rate close to 100%; for example, 10 grams of flakes + 10 grams of water, and then 40 grams of flour + 40 grams of water.

Mix the whole thing well. Then transfer the mixture into a jar and allow it to ferment. Sometimes you will have to feed the starter again several times before you see it becoming as active as before. This depends, among other things, on the room temperature and on the quality of the flour that you have chosen to feed it with.

4

DOUGH: THE KEY STEPS

The key steps in making the dough are the same across all the recipes, even if there are a few variations in some of them. We will take the production of a basic wild yeast bread dough as an example, as a way to understand the issues involved in each step. In the recipes themselves, you will find these steps presented throughout, but more briefly.

PRE-MIXING AND AUTOLYSIS

Everything starts with the mixing of flour and water (called *frasage* in French), an essential step in the production of bread dough.

Pour the water (or other liquid, depending on the recipe) into the bowl and add the flour. Mix briefly with a wooden spoon to hydrate the entire dough; there should be no dry flour left in the bowl. Cover it with a cloth or plastic wrap, and let it stand for at least 30 minutes. This resting period, called autolysis, will allow the gluten to relax and thus work on the texture of the dough and its toughness, while shortening the amount of time needed for kneading.

Worth Knowing

True autolysis involves only a mixture of water and flour. But in some recipes, the wild yeast starter is diluted in water before the flour is added, before the resting period. I prefer to call that "pseudo-autolysis." The advantage of this method, especially for beginners, is that the starter is already incorporated into the dough from the beginning. Thus, we skip a step, since all that remains is to incorporate the salt during kneading.

ADDING THE STARTER

After the first step, it is time to add the wild yeast starter. There are two options for incorporating the starter into the dough: you can either add it manually (using your wet hands or a wooden spoon) or use a dough mixer.

Your choice of technique will depend on the hydration of the dough and your own experience. For some very soft and sticky doughs, it will be much easier to use a dough mixer with a hook. The objective is not really to knead the dough, but rather to mix it briefly so that it is easier to handle later on.

INCORPORATING THE SALT

Depending on the recipe, the salt may or may not be added at the same time as the starter.

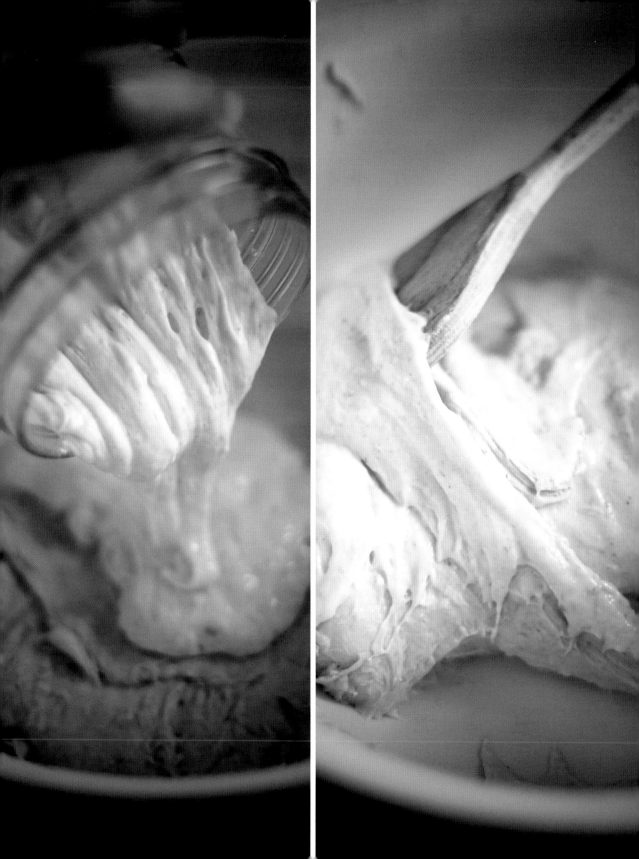

FIRST RISE AND FOLDS

The dough is now ready to ferment for the first time; this step is called bulk fermentation. Transfer the dough into a lightly greased large bowl or plastic container.

The first rise, or bulk fermentation, will usually take 3 to 4 hours. The time will vary depending on the recipe because it depends on the quantity of active starter being used. But it will also depend on the room temperature and the temperature of the ingredients, as we have already seen.

While the dough is resting in the bowl, you will make a series of folds (see photos, opposite) at 30- to 45-minute intervals, depending on the recipe. You will need to keep a container of water nearby. Wet your hand, and then catch up the dough at the edge of the bowl, stretch it out, and fold it over what was the top of the dough. Then rotate the bowl, make another fold, and continue in this manner until all of the dough has been stretched out and folded back on itself. Rewet your hand frequently so that the dough will not stick to your fingers. These folds help to develop the toughness of the dough while also aerating it. This technique will allow you to avoid using a dough mixer to knead the dough and will greatly improve the texture and elasticity.

You should be able to see a change in the texture as you go through the process of folding the dough during this bulk fermentation. It is important to make your folds more and more delicate the longer the dough has been resting to avoid discharging and breaking up the glutinous network.

Once the dough has fermented, its texture should be soft and airy. If it seems as though the dough needs to develop a little longer, especially at cold temperatures, it is better to let it ferment for at least an additional hour.

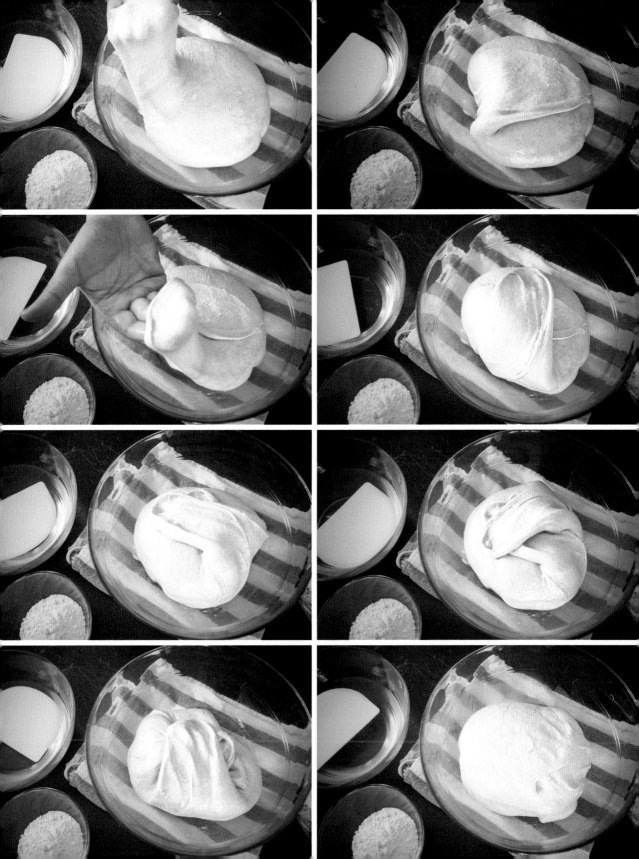

PRE-SHAPING AND RELAXATION

Once the dough is ready, it has to be detailed and pre-shaped. It is important not to neglect this step; not only does it allow for a successful final shaping, but it also guarantees the optimal development of the bread and an airy crumb.

Start by turning the dough out onto your work surface. Take care not to flour the surface too heavily. I use a scoop or a teaspoon filled with flour because that makes it possible to lay down a thin film without a lot of excess. Then, using a dough scraper or a spatula, gently peel the edges of the dough away from the bowl and let it drop onto your work surface.

Lightly flour the top of the dough and detail it as needed. Most of the recipes in this book will produce two medium loaves or one large one. This is usually determined by the number of bannetons or proofing baskets that you have available. Using a pastry cutter, divide the dough in half (for example) and lightly round it. You can lightly flour both your hand and the pastry cutter, especially if the dough is too sticky, and make rotating movements to make the dough into the shape of a ball, the idea being to pre-shape it before it relaxes.

After this pre-shaping step, it is important to let the dough relax and recover from the stress it has been subjected to. This will greatly ease the shaping step and allow for greater extensibility of the dough.

A SMALL TIP

To make this pre-shaping step easier, you can also use a pastry oil mister. Spray the pastry cutter and your hands lightly before pre-shaping. This can be very useful when you are just starting out and it is hard to handle a sticky dough.

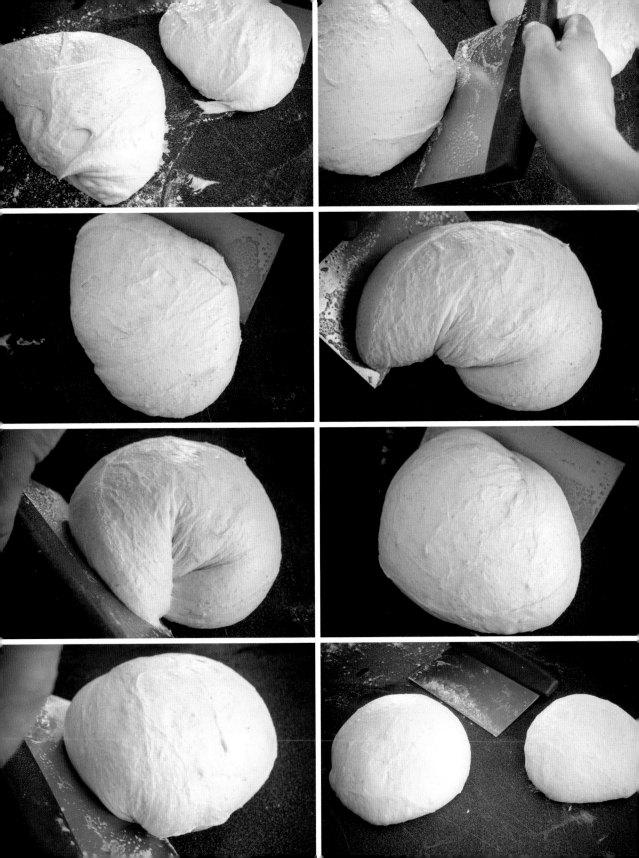

SHAPING

The dough is now relaxed and ready to be shaped. Whether you want to make a round loaf or a long, thin bâtard bread, dough that has relaxed is much easier to handle. To shape it, using a pastry cutter, lift the relaxed dough in a quick, sharp motion and turn it over onto the work surface so that the side that was underneath during the relaxation phase is now on top, facing you.

Depending on how you want to shape the loaf, pull the edges of the dough either toward the center or into a wallet shape. The following photos show the various stages of shaping the loaf.

After the dough is shaped, place it into a floured banneton (ideally floured with rice flour) so that the seam is on the top. Now the dough is ready for its second fermentation.

Shaping for a Round Banneton

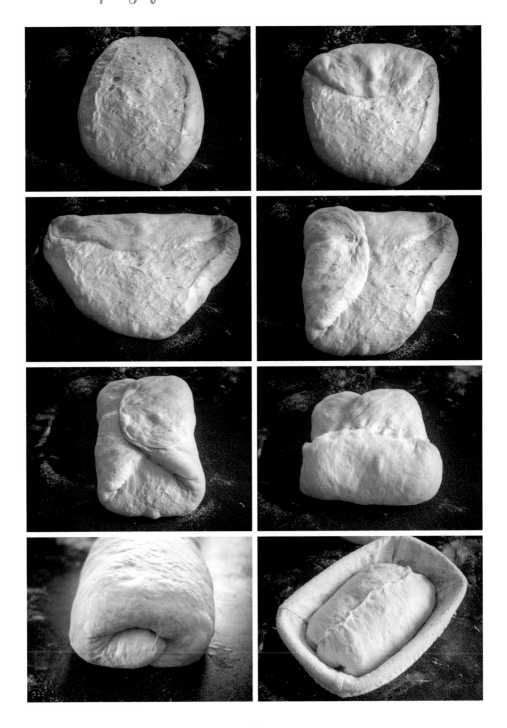

SECOND RISE

The second fermentation, or second rise, can take place either at room temperature or in the refrigerator, or using a combination of the two. Once the bread dough has been shaped and placed in the banneton, cover it with plastic wrap and let it stand for several hours, depending on the recommendations in the recipe.

At room temperature, the dough will rise faster, especially if it is hot. If you want to slow down the rise—for example, if you want it to happen overnight so that you can start the next day—all you have to do is refrigerate the banneton. You can also let the dough rise for an hour at room temperature and then put it in the refrigerator to slow it down until the following day.

Depending on your constraints, and the time at which you want to bake your bread, you can thus slow down the rising by 12 to 24 hours. As you experiment more and more, you can try out longer rest times and see how that affects the taste and texture of the bread. This experimentation will allow you to refine and adapt your method and, most of all, to learn a lot!

SCORING AND CUSTOMIZATION

Scoring your bread is a way to put your signature on it, but it is also a useful technique. It creates weak spots in the loaf that will allow gases to escape during baking without the entire loaf exploding.

Scoring or scarifying your bread is done with a bread scorer, a razor blade, or failing that, a small, sharp knife. It should be done in a quick, firm motion, especially if the dough is soft. For a cleaner scarification, you can take the dough, which has been rising at room temperature, and put it into the refrigerator for a few minutes; this will make its surface easier to score. Before putting the bread in the oven, place a sheet of parchment paper over the banneton, and potentially also a plate on top of that to make it easier, and turn the whole thing over so that the bread is now sitting on the parchment paper with the seam underneath, ready to be scored.

You can create different designs, depending on your taste (see the examples on the facing page). The best-known scoring designs are the baguette pattern, polka dots, or a herringbone pattern. One benefit of making your own bread is also that you can let your imagination run free, creating waves for a striped effect; using patterns like ears of wheat; or using a stencil, sprinkling the top of the loaf with cocoa or flour and then using a few cuts with the scorer to create your pattern. There are countless ideas you can explore to add visual pleasure to the pleasure of your palate!

BAKING

As we saw in chapter 2, "Utensils," the most convenient and efficient way to bake bread is to use a cast-iron baking dish. The steam that is released during baking, especially during the first few minutes, slows down the formation of the crust and thereby allows the bread to develop better.

Preheat the baking dish: put the dish, with its lid on, in the oven for 30 minutes before you start baking, in an oven heated to about 480°F (250°C). Make sure to wear oven gloves that are thick enough to prevent burns.

Once the dough is scarified, it is ready to be put into the oven. Transfer it into the baking dish and cover it; bake it covered for about 20 minutes. Then remove the cover and bake for another 20 minutes.

If you are baking on a baking stone, the principle is the same. You need to heat the stone at the same time as you heat the oven: place the stone on the rack and position the drip pan below so that you will be able to pour water onto it as soon as you start baking.

The bread should become nice and golden. Personally, I prefer it caramelized, with an extended baking time and a very brown crust!

Remove the bread from the dish and set it onto a cooling rack; allow it to cool completely before cutting it, even though the temptation to taste it while it's hot is always very strong.

5

BREADS LEAVENED EXCLUSIVELY WITH WILD YEAST STARTER:

RECIPES

Wild yeast bread is something you'll never get tired of! You can decorate it, personalize it, and create a multitude of varieties, from the simplest to the most elaborate. What do they all have in common? Slow rising, allowing exceptional aromas to be revealed that you can revel in every day.

THE BASIC RECIPE

This recipe will allow you to practice easily with few ingredients: white wheat flour, water, active wild yeast starter, and salt. These are basic ingredients for making your wild yeast bread, but the whole point of the recipe is to experiment with the amount of water that you use, in order to determine the optimal quantity to add so that the dough will be sufficiently hydrated, and especially so that you will feel comfortable with handling and shaping the dough.

The quantity of water given in this recipe is intended as a guideline. It always depends on the quality of the flour and your ability to handle a very soft dough. You should always start with a small amount of water, then add more gradually, so that you have time to familiarize yourself with the dough and, especially, to master your grasp of the ingredients. This will keep you from ending up with a mass of dough that is impossible to shape, which could just frustrate you.

For example, if you know that you absolutely want to produce a very airy crumb, like the ones you see on Instagram or other social media, where seasoned baking hobbyists display photographs of bread with crumbs full of air pockets, which they achieve by experimenting with hydration rates that sometimes go beyond 100% (i.e., more water than flour), then you can certainly reproduce those recipes. But first, you will have to take the time to experiment for yourself and, above all, to try out various kinds of flour. There is absolutely no point in trying this kind of hydration rate with a flour whose optimal rate is, for example, 70%.

In addition, you can certainly obtain a soft, airy crumb while staying within a perfectly acceptable hydration rate, and without it turning into a nightmare when you get to the point of shaping the dough; it is all a question of finding the middle ground.

Adopting this methodology for each of the recipes in this book is the best way to improve your technique and obtain a satisfactory result every time. As soon as you have gotten a good feeling for the use of a particular flour, you have mastered hydration, and the dough is reasonably easy to shape, you can experiment more easily!

Ingredients in weights and percentages
100 g of active wild yeast starter (20%)
280 to 350 g of water (56% to 70%)
500 g of high-gluten wheat flour (100%)
10 g of salt (2%)

Ingredients	In percentages	Weight in grams
Flour	100	500
Water	70	350
Salt	2	10
Liquid starter	20	100

The steps listed below are explained in detail in chapter 4, "Dough: The Key Steps."

Pre-mix and autolysis: Pour the water and flour into a large bowl and quickly mix with a spoon to combine them. Let the mixture stand for 60 minutes of autolysis.

Adding the starter: Add the wild yeast starter by mixing it into the dough with a wooden spoon or by using a dough mixer. Knead for 2 or 3 minutes until the starter is completely incorporated.

Cover it with a cloth and let it stand again for 30 to 40 minutes.

Note
Stop kneading as soon as the starter is incorporated. What you want is just to add it in, without developing gluten.

Incorporating the salt: Distribute the salt over the entire surface of the dough, and then knead to incorporate the salt. If you are kneading by hand, wet your hands first. Fold the edges of the dough over the salt while turning the bowl; there is no benefit in kneading the dough too much at this point (no more than a minute) because the salt will be distributed gradually during the folds in the following step.

First rise and folds: Transfer the dough to a clean bowl or a plastic container and round it lightly with wet hands. At this point, make a note of the time, because you will need to allow the dough to stand for 3 to 4 hours, on average. During this time, fold the dough at regular intervals (for example, once every 30 minutes for the first 2 hours).

Division and pre-shaping: Turn the dough out onto your lightly floured work surface and pre-shape it right away to make one large loaf (or, using a pastry cutter, divide the dough in half to make two medium loaves). Gently round the dough using the pastry cutter.

Relaxation and shaping: Let the dough ball(s) stand for 15 minutes at room temperature before working on them. Shape them into round loaves or into long, thin bâtard loaves, or any other shape you desire.

Second rise: Let the dough stand in bannetons for another 3 to 6 hours, depending on the room temperature, or put them into the refrigerator to slow down the process overnight.

Scoring: Turn the loaves out onto a peel or a plate covered with parchment paper. Score them using a bread scorer or a razor blade.

Baking: Transfer the dough into a baking dish that has been preheated for 30 minutes in the oven at about 480°F (250°C). Then bake covered for 20 minutes. Uncover the dish and bake for another 20 minutes.

Remove the bread from the dish and let it cool completely before slicing it.

FRUIT AND CHOCOLATE MUESLI BREAD

Ingredients

100 g of active starter

320 to 360 g of water

375 g of type T65 (high-gluten) flour

125 g of multigrain flour

10 g of salt

50 g of fruit muesli

50 g of chocolate chips

STEPS

Pre-mix and autolysis: Pour the water and the two kinds of flour into a large bowl. Then mix quickly with a spoon to thoroughly combine. Let stand for a 45-minute autolysis.

Adding the starter: Add the starter by mixing it into the dough using a wooden spoon or a dough mixer. Knead until the starter is completely incorporated.

Cover with a cloth and let stand for another 30 to 40 minutes.

Incorporating the salt: Add the salt and knead until it is well integrated into the dough.

First rise, adding the muesli and chocolate chips, folds: Lightly round the dough with wet hands. Cover and let stand for 2 to 4 hours, depending on the room temperature. After a 45-minute rest, distribute the muesli and the chocolate chips over the surface of the dough, pressing them in. Make a first fold. Make two more folds at 45-minute intervals.

Dividing and pre-shaping: Turn the dough out onto your lightly floured work surface and divide the dough into two balls using the pastry cutter. Pre-shape, without pressing too hard.

Relaxation and shaping: Let the dough stand for 15 to 20 minutes at room temperature. Shape it into round or rectangular loaves. Transfer the loaves into bannetons floured with rice flour.

Second rise: Let the dough stand for another 3 to 6 hours, depending on the room temperature, or put it into the refrigerator to slow down the process overnight.

Scoring: Turn the loaves out onto a piece of parchment paper and score them as you see fit.

Baking: Quickly transfer the dough into a baking dish that has been preheated for 30 minutes in the oven at about 480°F (250°C). Bake covered for 20 minutes. Uncover the dish and bake for another 15 minutes. Monitor the bread starting with the second baking phase; it should be properly golden.

CHEESE, THYME, AND OLIVE BREAD

Ingredients

100 g of active starter

330 to 365 g of water

150 g of multigrain flour

380 g of type T65 (high-gluten) wheat flour

1/2 tsp of dried thyme

80 g of finely diced cheese of your choice (Gouda, Emmentaler, Comté)

Black pitted olives (to taste)

STEPS

Autolysis: Pour the water, the thyme, and the two kinds of flour into a large bowl. Mix quickly with a wooden spoon to thoroughly combine. Let stand for a 45- to 60-minute autolysis.

Adding the starter: Add the starter by mixing it into the dough using a wooden spoon or a dough mixer. Knead until the starter is completely incorporated.

Cover with a cloth and let stand for another 20 minutes.

Incorporating the salt: Add the salt and knead until it is well integrated into the dough.

First rise, adding the cheese and olives, folds: Lightly round the dough with wet hands. Cover and let stand for 2 to 4 hours, depending on the room temperature.

After a 45-minute rest, distribute the cheese cubes and the pitted olives over the surface of the dough.

Make a first fold. Make three more folds at 30-minute intervals.

Division and pre-shaping: Turn the dough out onto your lightly floured work surface. Then use a pastry cutter to divide the dough into two dough balls, or leave as is to make a large loaf. Pre-shape, without pressing too hard.

Relaxation and shaping: Let the dough stand at room temperature for 20 to 25 minutes. Shape it into round or rectangular loaves. Transfer them into bannetons floured with rice flour.

Second rise: Let the dough stand for another 3 to 6 hours, depending on the room temperature, or put it into the refrigerator to slow down the process overnight.

Scoring: Transfer the dough onto a piece of parchment paper. Score as you see fit.

Baking: Quickly transfer the dough into a baking dish that has been preheated for 30 minutes in the oven at about 480°F (250°C). Bake covered for 20 minutes. Uncover the dish and bake for another 15 minutes. Monitor the bread starting with the second baking phase; it should be properly golden.

MULTI-SEED BARLEY BREAD

Ingredients

100 g of active starter

320 to 350 g of water

75 g of whole-grain barley flour

400 g of type T65 (high-gluten) wheat flour

40 g of fine durum wheat semolina

75 g of mixed seeds (sesame, poppy, flax, sunflower)

70 g of water for soaking the seeds

10 g of salt

STEPS

Preparing the seeds: In a frying pan, lightly toast the seeds for several minutes, watching carefully so that they do not burn. Pour them into a bowl and add the 70 grams of water. Let them soak until the seeds have absorbed all the liquid. Set aside.

Autolysis: Pour the water, the two kinds of flour, and the fine semolina into a large bowl. Mix quickly with a wooden spoon to thoroughly combine. Let stand for a 45-minute autolysis.

Adding the starter: Add the starter by mixing it into the dough using a wooden spoon or a dough mixer with a kneading hook. Knead until the starter is completely incorporated.

Stop kneading, cover with a cloth, and let stand for another 20 minutes.

Incorporating the salt: Add the salt and knead again until it is well integrated into the dough.

First rise, adding the seeds, and folds: Lightly round the dough with wet hands, cover, and let stand for 2 to 4 hours, depending on the room temperature. After 30 minutes of rest, distribute the soaked seeds over the surface of the dough, and then make a first fold. Make three more folds at 30-minute intervals.

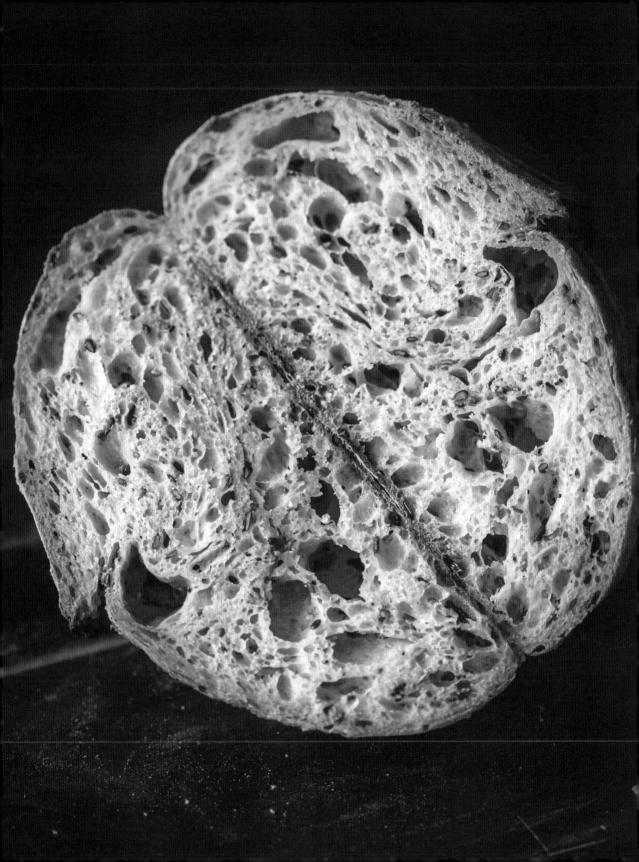

Dividing and pre-shaping: Using a pastry cutter, divide the dough into two balls, or leave as is to make one large loaf; pre-shape, without pressing too hard.

Relaxation and shaping: Let the dough stand for 20 to 25 minutes at room temperature. Then shape it into round or rectangular loaves and place it into bannetons floured with rice flour.

Second rise: Let stand for another 3 to 6 hours, depending on the room temperature, or put it into the refrigerator to slow down the process overnight.

Scoring: Transfer the dough to a piece of parchment paper and score it as you see fit.

Baking: Quickly transfer the dough into a baking dish that has been preheated for 30 minutes in the oven at about 480°F (250°C). Bake covered for 20 minutes. Uncover the dish and continue to bake for another 20 minutes.

CIABATTA

Ingredients

150 g of active starter

350 to 380 g of water

500 g of pizza flour (or if unavailable, gluten-rich flour)

35 g of olive oil

10 g of salt

STEPS

Autolysis: Pour the water and flour into a large bowl, and then mix quickly with a wooden spoon to thoroughly combine. Let stand for a 60-minute autolysis.

Adding the starter: Add the starter by mixing it into the dough using a wooden spoon or a dough mixer with a kneading hook. Knead until the starter is completely incorporated.

Cover with a cloth and let stand for another 20 minutes.

Incorporating the salt: Add the salt and knead again until it is well integrated into the dough.

Rise and folds: Transfer the dough, which will be sticky, into a greased bowl, cover, and let stand for 3 to 4 hours, depending on the room temperature.

During the resting period, make four folds at 30-minute intervals, using olive oil at each fold to oil your hands and keep the dough from sticking to your fingers.

Dividing: To make it easier to divide the dough and allow the flavors to develop, transfer the dough into an airtight oiled container and let stand in the refrigerator overnight.

The next day, turn the dough out onto a floured work surface, flour the top of the dough, and divide it into three rectangles using your pastry cutter. Place them on parchment paper.

Baking: Preheat the baking stone in the oven, along with the drip pan, at about 480°F (250°C) for at least 30 minutes. Transfer the dough from the parchment paper to a peel (or a tray). Then, with a quick motion, slide it onto the hot stone. At the same time, pour a small glassful of water into the drip pan and immediately close the oven door.

Bake each ciabatta for 20 minutes; the bread should sound hollow when it is done.

Remove from the oven, let it cool on a wire rack, and then make delicious sandwiches!

ZUCCHINI-PARMESAN BREAD

Ingredients

100 g of active starter

320 to 360 g of water

550 g of type T65 (high-gluten) wheat flour

200g of grated, drained zucchini

120 g of grated parmesan

10 g of salt

STEPS

Preparation of the zucchini: Start by grating the zucchini, putting them in a cloth, and squeezing them to eliminate as much water as possible. Set aside.

Autolysis: Pour the water and flour into a large bowl. Mix quickly with a wooden spoon to thoroughly combine. Let stand for a 60-minute autolysis.

Adding the starter: Add the starter by mixing it into the dough using a wooden spoon or a dough mixer with a kneading hook. Knead until the starter is completely incorporated.

Stop kneading, cover with a cloth, and let stand for another 10 minutes.

Incorporating the salt: Add the salt and knead until it is well integrated into the dough.

First rise, adding the parmesan and zucchini, folds: Lightly round the dough with wet hands, put it into a container, and cover. Let stand for 2 to 4 hours at room temperature.

After 45 minutes of rest, distribute the parmesan and the zucchini over the entire surface of the dough.

Make a first fold. Then make three more folds at 30-minute intervals.

Dividing and pre-shaping: Turn the dough out onto your lightly floured work surface. Then divide the dough, using a pastry cutter, into two dough balls, or leave as is to make one large loaf. Pre-shape, without pressing too hard.

Relaxation and shaping: Let the dough stand for 20 minutes at room temperature before shaping it into a round or rectangular loaf or loaves. Transfer into bannetons floured with rice flour.

Second rise: Let stand for another 3 to 4 hours, depending on the room temperature, or put in the refrigerator to slow down the process overnight.

Scoring: Transfer the dough to a piece of parchment paper. Score as you see fit.

Baking: Quickly transfer into a baking dish that has been heated for 30 minutes at about 480°F (250°C). Bake covered for 20 minutes. Uncover the dish and bake for another 20 minutes.

SEMOLINA BREAD
(WITH FRUIT YEAST)

Ingredients

125 g of active (fruit) starter

330 to 370 g of water

230 g of fine durum wheat semolina

270 g of type T65 (high-gluten) wheat flour

40 g of sweet butter at room temperature

10 g of salt

STEPS

Autolysis: Pour the water, the flour, and the semolina into a large bowl. Mix briefly with a wooden spoon to thoroughly combine. Let stand for an autolysis of 60 to 120 minutes.

Adding the starter: Add the fruit-based starter by mixing it into the dough using a wooden spoon or a dough mixer with a kneading hook. Knead until the starter is completely incorporated.

Cover with a cloth and let stand for another 20 minutes.

Incorporating the salt and butter: Add the salt and knead again. Then incorporate the butter while continuing to knead so that the result will be nicely uniform.

First rise and folds: Lightly round the dough with wet hands, cover, and let rise for 2 to 4 hours, depending on the room temperature, making a series of four folds, one every 30 minutes.

Dividing and pre-shaping: Turn the dough out onto your lightly floured work surface. Then, using the pastry cutter, divide it into two balls, or leave as is to make one large loaf. Pre-shape, without pressing too hard.

Relaxation and shaping: Let the dough stand for 20 to 25 minutes at room temperature. Shape into a round or rectangular loaf or loaves. Put into bannetons floured with rice flour.

Second rise: Let the dough stand for another 3 to 4 hours, depending on the room temperature, or put into the refrigerator to rest overnight.

Scoring: Turn the dough out onto a piece of parchment paper and score as you see fit.

Baking: Quickly transfer the dough into a baking dish that has been preheated for 30 minutes in the oven at about 480°F (250°C). Bake covered for 20 minutes. Uncover the dish and bake for another 15 minutes. Monitor the bread starting with the second baking phase; it should be properly golden!

Option
Scatter black cumin seeds into each incision right after scoring the dough.

CHALLAH

Ingredients

200 g of active starter

125 g of warm water

80 ml of oil

150 g of eggs (3 eggs)

40 g of powdered sugar

600 g of all-purpose wheat flour

11 g of salt

Glaze (see below) and sesame seeds

STEPS

Preparation of the dough: Pour the warm water, the eggs, and the oil into the bowl of the dough mixer, and then add the starter, stirring it in as you add it. Then add the flour, salt, and sugar, and start kneading until the dough is smooth and uniform and begins to peel away from the sides of the bowl.

First rise: Transfer the dough into a lightly oiled bowl, cover with plastic wrap, and let it rise at room temperature for 3 to 5 hours.

Division and shaping: Turn the dough out onto a floured work surface. Using a pastry cutter, divide the dough into two halves. Then make each half into a braid, or else take the whole dough and divide it into six portions to make one large braid with six strands.

Set the braided loaf or loaves on a tray covered with parchment paper.

Second rise: Let it rise for another 4 to 6 hours, depending on the room temperature.

Glaze and baking: Preheat the oven to about 400°F (200°C). Before baking, brush the bread with the glaze (an egg beaten with 1 tablespoon of water) and sprinkle with sesame seeds. Put it in the oven and lower the temperature to about 350°F (180°C). Bake for 30 to 45 minutes depending on the size of the bread.

If the braid is starting to brown too quickly, place a piece of aluminum foil over it while baking and continue.

CARROT-PAPRIKA BREAD

Ingredients

100 g of active starter

300 to 350 g of carrot juice

450 g of type T65 (high-gluten) wheat flour

50 g of type T150 (dark whole wheat) flour

1/2 tsp of ground paprika

10 g of salt

STEPS

Autolysis: Pour the carrot juice, paprika, and the two kinds of flour into a large bowl. Mix briefly with a wooden spoon to thoroughly combine. Let stand for an autolysis of 45 to 60 minutes.

Adding the starter: Add the starter by mixing it into the dough using a wooden spoon or a dough mixer with a kneading hook. Knead until the starter is completely incorporated.

Cover with a cloth and let stand for another 20 minutes.

Incorporating the salt: Add the salt and knead again until it is well integrated into the dough.

First rise and folds: Lightly round the dough with wet hands, cover, and let it stand for 2 to 4 hours, depending on the room temperature. Make four folds during the resting period, at 30-minute intervals.

Dividing and pre-shaping: Divide the dough into two halves with the pastry cutter, or leave as is to make one large loaf. Pre-shape, without pressing too hard.

Relaxation and shaping: Let the dough stand for 20 to 25 minutes at room temperature. Then form a round or rectangular loaf or loaves. Transfer into bannetons floured with rice flour.

Second rise: Let stand for another 3 to 4 hours, depending on the room temperature, or put it into the refrigerator to slow down the process overnight.

Scoring: Transfer the dough to a piece of parchment paper and score as you see fit.

Baking: Quickly transfer the dough into a baking dish that has been preheated for 30 minutes in the oven at about 480°F (250°C). Bake covered for 20 minutes. Uncover the dish and bake for another 20 minutes.

PAVÉ LOAF WITH A HINT OF RYE

Ingredients

100 g of active starter

320 to 350 g of water

450 g of high-gluten wheat flour

25 g of dark whole wheat flour

25 g of rye flour

10 g of salt

STEPS

Autolysis: Pour the water and the various kinds of flour into a large bowl. Mix quickly with a wooden spoon to thoroughly combine. Let stand for a 60-minute autolysis.

Adding the starter: Add the starter by mixing it into the dough using a wooden spoon or a dough mixer with a kneading hook. Knead until the starter is completely incorporated.

Cover with a cloth and let stand for another 20 minutes.

Incorporating the salt: Add the salt and knead until it is well integrated into the dough.

Rise and folds: Cover the bowl and let it stand 3 to 4 hours, depending on the room temperature. During the resting period, make four folds at 30-minute intervals.

Transfer the dough into an oiled or airtight container and put it into the refrigerator overnight or for up to 18 hours. This will allow the dough to develop a lot of flavor.

Dividing: The next day, turn the dough out onto a floured work surface, being careful not to flatten it. Lightly flour the top and use a pastry cutter to divide it into medium-sized slabs to make pavé loaves.

Scoring: Transfer the pavé loaves onto a piece of parchment paper and scarify each loaf with a stroke of the blade.

Baking: Quickly transfer the dough into a baking dish that has been preheated for 30 minutes in the oven at about 480°F (250°C), along with the drip pan. At the same time, pour a small glassful of water into the drip pan and then immediately close the oven door.

Bake each loaf for 20 minutes; the bread should sound hollow and look nicely golden.

When you take it out of the oven, let it cool on a wire rack.

TURMERIC AND BLACK CUMIN BREAD

Ingredients

200 g of active starter

300 to 350 g of water

500 g of type T65 (high-gluten) wheat flour

3 tablespoons of powdered curcuma

3 tablespoons of black cumin seeds

10 g of salt

STEPS

Autolysis: Pour the water, turmeric, and flour into a large bowl. Mix briefly with a wooden spoon to thoroughly combine. Let stand for a 30- to 60-minute autolysis.

Adding the starter: Add the starter by mixing it into the dough using a wooden spoon or a dough mixer with a kneading hook. Knead until the starter is completely incorporated.

Cover with a cloth and let stand for another 20 minutes.

Incorporating the salt: Add the salt and knead again until it is well integrated into the dough.

First rise and folds: Lightly round the dough with wet hands, cover, and let stand for 2 to 3 hours, depending on the room temperature. Make a first fold after 30 minutes, adding the black cumin seeds, and then three more folds at 45-minute intervals.

Transfer the dough into a greased container, fold down one last time, and put into the refrigerator overnight.

Dividing and pre-shaping: The next day, turn the dough out onto a work surface. Divide it into two halves with the pastry cutter, or leave it as is to make one large loaf. Pre-shape, without pressing too hard.

Relaxation and shaping: Let the dough stand for 15 minutes at room temperature. Then shape it into round or rectangular loaves. Place it into bannetons floured with rice flour.

Second rise: Let the dough stand again for 3 to 4 hours, depending on the room temperature, or put it into the refrigerator to slow down the process overnight.

Scoring: Transfer the loaf or loaves to a piece of parchment paper and score as you see fit.

Baking: Quickly transfer the dough into a baking dish that has been preheated for 30 minutes in the oven at about 480°F (250°C). Bake covered for 20 minutes. Uncover the dish and bake for another 20 minutes.

PROVENÇAL LOAF

Ingredients

100 g of active starter

300 to 350 g of water

450 g of type T65 (high-gluten) wheat flour

50 g of whole wheat flour

30 g of oil-free dried tomatoes, chopped into small pieces

1 tablespoon of dried oregano, thyme, and basil mix

10 g of salt

STEPS

Autolysis: Pour the water, herbs, and two kinds of flour into a large bowl. Mix briefly with a wooden spoon to thoroughly combine. Let stand for a 40-minute autolysis.

Adding the starter: Add the starter by mixing it into the dough using a wooden spoon or a food processor with a kneading hook. Knead until the starter is completely incorporated.

Cover with a cloth and let stand for another 20 minutes.

Incorporating the salt: Add the salt and knead again until it is well integrated into the dough.

First rise, adding the tomatoes, and folds: Lightly round the dough with wet hands. Cover and let stand for 2 to 3 hours, depending on the room temperature.

Make a first fold after 30 minutes, mixing in the chopped dried tomatoes. Then make three more folds at 45-minute intervals.

Dividing and pre-shaping: Turn the dough out onto the work surface and either divide it in half with the pastry cutter or leave it as is to make one large loaf. Pre-shape, without pressing too hard.

Relaxation and shaping: Let the dough stand for 15 minutes at room temperature before shaping it into a round or rectangular loaf or loaves. Put the loaves into bannetons floured with rice flour.

Second rise: Let the dough stand for another 3 to 4 hours, depending on the room temperature, or put it into the refrigerator to slow down the process overnight.

Scoring: Transfer the dough to a piece of parchment paper and score as you see fit.

Baking: Quickly transfer the dough into a baking dish that has been preheated for 30 minutes in the oven at about 480°F (250°C). Bake covered for 20 minutes. Uncover the dish and bake for another 20 minutes.

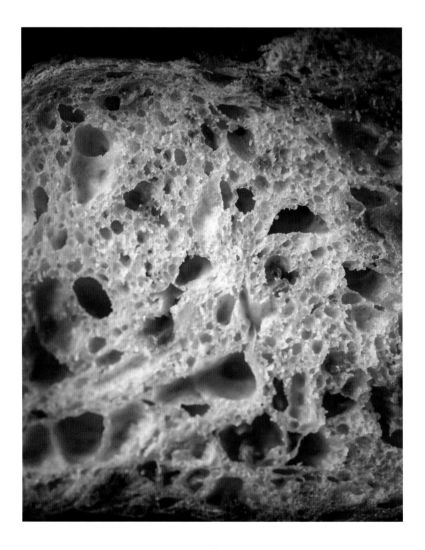

TAHINI AND KAMUT®
FLOUR BREAD

Ingredients

100 g of active starter

330 to 360 g of water

380 g of type T65 (high-gluten) wheat flour

120 g of Kamut® flour from Khorasan wheat

35 g of sesame paste (tahini)

10 g of salt

STEPS

Autolysis: Pour the water and the two kinds of flour into a large bowl. Mix briefly with a wooden spoon to thoroughly combine. Let stand for an autolysis of 60 to 90 minutes.

Adding the starter and the sesame paste: Add the starter and the sesame paste by mixing them into the dough with a wooden spoon or using a food processor with a kneading hook. Knead until the starter is completely incorporated.

Cover with a cloth and let stand for another 20 minutes.

Incorporating the salt: Add the salt and knead until it is well integrated into the dough.

First rise and folds: Lightly round the dough with wet hands. Cover and let stand for 3 to 4 hours, depending on the room temperature. During this resting period, make four folds at 30-minute intervals.

Dividing and pre-shaping: Either divide the dough in half with the pastry cutter or leave it as is to make one large loaf. Pre-shape, without pressing too hard.

Relaxation and shaping: Let the dough stand for 20 minutes at room temperature. Shape it into round or rectangular loaves. Transfer the loaves into bannetons floured with rice flour.

WILD YEAST TORTILLAS

Ingredients

100 g of active starter

140 to 160 g of warm water

225 g of type T65 (high-gluten) wheat flour

75 g of type T150 (dark whole wheat) wheat flour

25 g of oil

5 g of salt

STEPS

Preparing the dough: In a large bowl, dissolve the starter in the warm water, add the two kinds of flour, and mix briefly with a spoon without kneading. Let the mixture stand for 45 minutes.

Add the salt and oil and knead until they are well incorporated.

First rise: Lightly round the dough with wet hands. Cover and let stand for 3 to 5 hours, depending on the room temperature.

Dividing, shaping, and relaxation: Turn the dough out onto a lightly floured work surface and divide it into several tangerine-sized portions.

Gradually round the balls of dough, and then cover with plastic wrap and let stand for 30 minutes at room temperature.

Baking: Heat a non-stick pan. Take a ball of dough, flour it, and then roll it out on a floured work surface. The tortilla should not stick to the work surface.

When the pan is very hot, put the tortillas into the pan one at a time and bake each one for one to two minutes on each side.

So that the tortillas do not dry out, put the finished tortillas under a cloth as you finish each one; at the end, store them in an airtight container.

50/50 BREAD

Ingredients

120 g of active starter

300 to 350 g of water

250 g of type T65 (high-gluten) wheat flour

250 g of type T150 dark whole stone-ground wheat flour

10 g of salt

STEPS

Autolysis: Pour the water and the two kinds of flour into a large bowl. Mix quickly with a wooden spoon to thoroughly combine. Let stand for a 60-minute autolysis.

Adding the starter: Add the starter by mixing it into the dough using a wooden spoon or a food processor with a kneading hook. Knead until the starter is completely incorporated.

Cover with a cloth and let stand for another 20 minutes.

Incorporating the salt: Add the salt and knead until it is well integrated into the dough.

First rise and folds: Lightly round the dough with wet hands. Cover and let stand for 2 to 3 hours, depending on the room temperature. During this resting period, make a series of four folds at 30-minute intervals.

Dividing and pre-shaping: Turn the dough out onto your lightly floured work surface. Divide the dough into two balls, using the pastry cutter, or leave as is to make one large loaf. Pre-shape, without pressing too hard.

Relaxation and shaping: Let the dough stand for 15 minutes at room temperature. Then shape it into round or rectangular loaves. Transfer the loaves into bannetons that have been floured with rice flour or lined with wheat, oat, or spelt flakes.

Second rise: Let the dough stand for another 3 to 4 hours, depending on the room temperature, or put it into the refrigerator to slow down the process overnight.

Scoring: Transfer the dough to a piece of parchment paper and score as you see fit.

Baking: Quickly transfer the dough into a baking dish that has been preheated for 30 minutes in the oven at about 480°F (250°C). Bake covered for 20 minutes. Remove the lid from the dish and continue baking for another 15 minutes.

OLD-FASHIONED MUSTARD BUNS

Ingredients

100 g of active starter

100 g of water

230 ml of warm water

25 g of powdered sugar

60 g of soft butter

500 g of all-purpose flour

10 g of salt

75 g of whole-grain mustard

Glaze and cheese (or sesame seeds) for the coating

STEPS

Preparing the dough: In the bowl of the food processor, begin by thinning the starter with the water. Then add the milk, sugar, flour, mustard, and salt. Knead for a few minutes, scraping the edges of the bowl if the ingredients do not fall back toward the kneading hook while you are kneading. Continue to knead, adding the soft butter; it should totally integrate into the dough.

If the dough is too soft, you can add a little bit of flour; it should be soft without being too sticky.

First rise: Transfer the dough into a greased recipient and lightly round. Let it stand for 3 to 4 hours, depending on the room temperature, and make three folds at 45-minute intervals.

You can then allow the dough to stand in an airtight container until the next day, if you want to.

Dividing and shaping: Turn the dough out onto a floured work surface. Divide the dough into several portions of 100 grams each with a pastry cutter. Round each portion and deposit it on a tray covered with parchment paper as you go along. Cover with plastic wrap when all the portions are on the tray.

Second rise: Let the dough stand for another 3 to 5 hours, depending on the room temperature.

Coating: Brush the bread rolls with the glaze (an egg beaten with 1 tablespoon of water) and sprinkle with grated cheese or sesame seeds.

Baking: Preheat the oven to about 400°F (200°C). Put the dough into the oven and lower the temperature to about 350°F (180°C). Then bake for about 25 to 30 minutes. The loaves should be nicely golden.

Remove from the oven and sprinkle a little parsley on each roll. These buns are perfect for little burgers!

FLAXSEED BREAD

Ingredients

100 g of active starter

330 to 360 g of water

50 g of whole-wheat flour

450 g of type T65 (high-gluten) wheat flour

40 g of flaxseed

10 g of salt

STEPS

Chilled autolysis: Pour the water and the two kinds of flour, along with the flax-seed, into a large bowl. Mix briefly with a wooden spoon to thoroughly combine. Cover the bowl and put it into the refrigerator overnight.

Given how long the chilled autolysis will take, you can start it at the same time as you feed the starter, in order to then continue the preparation the following morning.

Adding the starter: The next day, add the active starter by mixing it into the dough using a wooden spoon or a food processor with a kneading hook. Knead until the starter is completely incorporated.

Cover with a cloth and let it stand for another 20 minutes.

Incorporating the salt: Add the salt and knead again until it is well integrated into the dough.

First rise and folds: Lightly round the dough with wet hands, cover, and let stand for 3 to 4 hours, depending on the room temperature. While it is resting, make four folds at 30-minute intervals.

Dividing and pre-shaping: Divide the dough into two balls, using the pastry cutter, or leave it as is to make one large loaf. Pre-shape, without pressing too hard.

Relaxation and shaping: Let the dough stand for 20 to 25 minutes at room temperature before shaping it into a round or rectangular loaf or loaves. Transfer them into bannetons floured with rice flour.

Second rise: Let the dough stand for another 3 to 6 hours, depending on the room temperature, or put it into the refrigerator to slow down the process overnight.

Scoring: Transfer the loaf or loaves to a piece of parchment paper and score them as you see fit.

Baking: Quickly transfer the dough into a baking dish that has been preheated for 30 minutes in the oven at about 480°F (250°C). Bake covered for 20 minutes. Uncover and bake for another 20 minutes.

FOUR-GRAIN
PRUNE BREAD

Ingredients

100 g of active starter

330 to 360 g of water

380 g of type T65 (high-gluten) wheat flour

60 g of type T150 (dark whole wheat) flour

40 g of rye flour

20 g of buckwheat flour

10 g of salt

5 or 6 pitted prunes, cut in half

STEPS

Autolysis: Pour the water and the flours into a large bowl. Mix briefly with a wooden spoon to thoroughly combine. Let stand for a 30-minute autolysis.

Adding the starter: Add the starter by mixing it into the dough using a wooden spoon or a food processor with a dough hook. Knead until the starter is completely incorporated.

Cover with a cloth and let stand for another 20 minutes.

Incorporating the salt: Add the salt and knead again until it is well integrated into the dough.

First rise and folds: Lightly round the dough with wet hands. Cover and let stand for 2 to 4 hours, depending on the room temperature. While it is rising, make a series of four folds at 30-minute intervals.

You can either add the prunes during the first fold or integrate them into the loaves during the shaping, while you are folding the dough at that point.

Dividing and pre-shaping: Turn the dough out onto your work surface and divide the dough into two balls, using the pastry cutter, or leave as is to make one large loaf.

Pre-shape, without pressing too hard.

Relaxation, adding the prunes, and shaping: Let the loaves stand at room temperature for 15 minutes. Then integrate pieces of prune into the loaves as you shape them into either round or rectangular loaves. Transfer them into bannetons floured with rice flour or lined with wheat, oat, or spelt flakes.

Second rise: Let the loaves stand for another 3 to 4 hours, depending on the room temperature, or put them into the refrigerator to slow down the process overnight.

Scoring: Turn the loaves out onto a piece of parchment paper and score them as you see fit.

Baking: Quickly transfer the dough into a baking dish that has been preheated for 30 minutes in the oven at about 480°F (250°C). Bake covered for 20 minutes. Uncover and bake for another 15 minutes.

When you take the bread out of the oven, let it cool on a wire rack.

WHOLE-GRAIN PITA BREAD

Ingredients

100 g of active starter

360 g of water

500 g of type T150 (dark whole wheat) stone-ground wheat flour

10 g of salt

STEPS

Autolysis: Pour the water and the flour into a large bowl. Mix quickly with a spoon to thoroughly combine. Let stand for a 45-minute autolysis.

Adding the starter: Place the bowl in the food processor with a kneading hook and add the starter. Knead until the starter is completely incorporated.

Cover with a cloth and let stand for another 30 to 40 minutes.

Incorporating the salt: Add the salt and knead again until it is well integrated into the dough.

First rise and folds: Lightly round the dough with wet hands. Cover and let stand for 2 to 3 hours. Make two folds at 30-minute intervals during the beginning of the rising time.

Dividing and shaping: Divide the dough into 6 to 8 portions, depending on how large you want your loaves to be, and quickly round them, generously flouring the loaves and the work surface.

Baking: Preheat the pizza stone in the oven at about 480°F (250°C)—or hotter, if your oven allows. Once the stone is heated, flatten each roll with a floured roller, and then place the flattened disc on the stone.

While it is baking, which will take only 5 to 7 minutes, the bread will inflate and take on the appearance of a ball.

When you take it out of the oven, place it directly on a cloth and cover it so that it will not dry out.

SEEDED MILLED RYE BREAD

Ingredients

125 g of active starter fed exclusively with rye the previous day

100 g of type T65 (high-gluten) white flour

120 g of rye flour

½ teaspoon of powdered malt (optional)

40 g of crushed rye grains

40 g of whole-grain wheat

300 g of water

85 g of mixed seeds (sunflower, squash, flax, sesame, etc.)

1 tablespoon of honey

6 g of salt

Oat or wheat flakes for the exterior

STEPS

Preparing the seeds: Dissolve the starter in the water. Pour in the wheat and rye grains and the seed mixture. Let soak for 8 to 12 hours.

Mixing: The next day, add the flours, honey, salt, and malt powder. Mix with a wooden spoon. Pour the mixture into a cake pan covered in parchment paper.

Spray a little water on top and sprinkle with the flakes.

Rise and baking: Let rise for 2 to 3 hours, depending on the room temperature, before baking it for 1 hour to 1 hour and 15 minutes in an oven preheated to about 345°F (175°C).

Take the bread out of the oven and let it stand for several hours before cutting. Ideally, wait until the next day to eat it.

CHILLED-AUTOLYSIS BAGUETTES

Ingredients

100 g of active starter

330 g of water

500 g of type T65 (high-gluten) wheat flour

10 g of salt

STEPS

Autolysis: Pour the water and flour into a large bowl. Mix quickly with a spoon to thoroughly combine. Let stand in the refrigerator overnight.

Adding the starter: The next day, transfer the dough into the bowl of the food processor and add the starter. Knead until the starter is completely incorporated.

Cover with a cloth and let stand for another 30 minutes.

Incorporating the salt: Add the salt and knead again until it is well integrated into the dough. Knead the dough until it is smooth and peels away from the sides of the bowl.

First rise and folds: Lightly round the dough and transfer it into a container, cover, and let it stand for 3 to 4 hours. While it is rising, make a series of three folds at 45-minute intervals.

Put the container back into the refrigerator and let it stand overnight.

Dividing and pre-shaping: Turn the dough out onto a work surface and divide it into portions of 230 to 250 grams each using the pastry cutter. This is lighter than a classic baguette to make it easier to bake it in a home oven on a medium-sized stone.

Lightly pre-shape, folding the dough over on itself.

Relaxation and shaping: Let the loaves stand, covered in plastic wrap, for 20 to 30 minutes. Using the pastry cutter, take up each loaf and shape it into a baguette, flattening it with the palm of your hand. Fold it over again, sealing the edges, then roll it and stretch it to create the baguette shape.

Second rise: Place the baguettes, with the seam facing up, on a floured surface. Let them stand for 1 1/2 hours.

Scoring: Turn the baguettes out onto a piece of parchment paper, with the seam facing down, and score them with a quick cut.

Baking: Preheat the stone in the oven for 45 minutes at about 480°F (250°C), along with the dripping pan. Then rapidly slide the baguettes onto the hot stone. At the same time, pour a glass of water into the dripping pan and immediately close the oven door. Bake each baguette for about 20 minutes.

Option
For a unique touch, add a little turmeric to the baguette dough.
It's guaranteed to impress!

TIP: WHAT IF I WANT TO USE A RECIPE FOR YEAST BREAD AND CONVERT IT?

Once you have an active wild yeast starter that you have some experience with, having experimented with it in several different bread recipes, you might want to have fun trying a recipe that was written using commercial yeast, converting it so that you only use wild yeast starter instead.

Everyone has their own different method for converting a commercial-yeast-based bread recipe into a wild yeast starter recipe. Theoretically, once you have mastered the hydration level of your starter, it should not be complicated to adapt any recipe based on yeast. The other important issue is the amount of commercial yeast used in the recipe.

Taking these two factors into consideration, it is easy to convert your favorite recipe into an "improved" wild yeast version.

Knowing that the recipe for wild yeast starter explained in this book, as well as all the bread recipes in the book, are based on a 100% hydration level for the starter, we begin with the information that the starter is made up of 50% water and 50% flour. Thus, we will simply need to take that into account as we adapt the recipe, reducing the quantities of flour and water called for in the original recipe, since the liquid starter already contains some flour and water.

I usually start by incorporating 20% of the recipe's flour weight in the liquid starter, and then I refine the quantities as I experiment with the recipe. For instance, in a recipe based on 1 kilogram of flour, I will add 200 grams of wild yeast starter. If the original yeast-based recipe requires 1 hour of rising time, I will try for about 3 to 4 hours of rising to begin with. And then, again, I adapt and refine the recipe as I experiment with it, based on the results I get.

6

THERE'S MORE THAN JUST BREAD!

At first, you start a wild yeast starter mainly in order to make bread, but did you know that you can use it in many different kinds of recipes? Sweet and salty both! Not only is it delicious, but you will also see that, depending on the recipe, you can use active starter or not, which will avoid waste if you have extra starter!

SOFT CARAMELIZED WAFFLES

Ingredients

200 g of active starter

275 g of type T55 (all-purpose) white flour

120 ml of milk

2 large eggs

160 g of melted butter

150 g of pearl sugar

1 pinch of salt

STEPS

1   Start by using a wooden spoon to mix the starter, the flour, and the milk. The batter might seem a little dry, but that is totally normal. Let it stand for 2 to 3 hours, depending on the room temperature; the batter should double in volume.

2   Transfer the fermented batter into the bowl of a food processor equipped with a flat beater. Add the eggs, along with the pinch of salt, and start mixing. At first, it will seem like the batter is not becoming homogenized, like a puff pastry batter, but as you keep beating it, it will become smoother and more uniform.

3   Once the eggs are incorporated, gradually add the melted butter, beating continually the whole time. Increase the speed of the food processor to make the batter nicely uniform.

4   Using a spoon or a rubber spatula, incorporate the pearl sugar.

5   Preheat the waffle iron and put in a little bit of the batter, using a tablespoon; close the waffle iron and keep an eye on the baking. The waffles should come out golden and caramelized.

When taking the waffles out of the waffle iron, be careful not to burn yourself on the caramel, which will still be boiling hot. Use two forks to unstick them, and let them cool down a little before eating them.

DRIED APRICOT SEEDCAKE

Ingredients

120 g of starter (active or inactive)

150 g of type T65 (high-gluten) white flour

50 g of spelt flour

225 ml of unsweetened concentrated milk

2 large eggs

120 g of melted butter

100 g of powdered sugar

25 g of your choice of mixed seeds (flax seeds, poppy seeds, sesame seeds, etc.)

6 or 7 dried apricots

2 teaspoons of baking powder

1 teaspoon vanilla extract

STEPS

1   Preheat the oven to about 400°F (200°C).

2   In a bowl, dilute the starter in the unsweetened concentrated milk, add the eggs, and mix well. Then incorporate the powdered sugar and the vanilla.

3   Separately, mix the two kinds of flour, the seeds, the salt, and the baking powder.

4   Combine the two mixtures and beat; the batter should be nicely uniform. Pour in the melted butter while continuing to beat to thoroughly incorporate it.

5   Finally, add the dried apricots, finely diced, and mix well.

6   Pour the batter into a buttered cake pan and put it into the preheated oven for 10 minutes. After 10 minutes, lower the temperature to about 345°F (175°C) and bake for another 30 to 40 minutes.

The cake should be golden. Check that it is done by inserting a toothpick into the center; it should come out clean, without any traces of raw batter.

ULTRA-SOFT PECAN BROWNIES

Ingredients

150 g of active or inactive starter

200 g of dark baking chocolate

2 large eggs

130 g of powdered sugar

125 g of butter

100 g of chocolate chips

100 g of chopped pecans

1 pinch of salt

STEPS

1 Chop the baking chocolate, dice the butter, and put them into a bowl. Melt them in a microwave oven.

2 Add the sugar and mix well. Then incorporate the eggs, one at a time, and finish by adding in the starter and a pinch of salt. Mix well to create a smooth, uniform batter.

3 Using a wooden spoon, mix in the chocolate chips and the chopped pecans.

4 Pour the batter into a greased pan and bake at about 350°F (180°C) for about 20 minutes. The brownies should still be gooey.

MINI JAM BRIOCHES

Ingredients

500 g of oatmeal flour

185 g of active starter

100 g of powdered sugar

4 large eggs

80 ml of warm milk

225 g of room-temperature butter

2 teaspoons of vanilla extract

7 g of salt

Filling: Your choice of jam

Glaze: 1 egg + 1 tablespoon of water

STEPS

1   Pour the warm milk and the active starter into the food processor bowl and mix well with a spoon or a spatula.

2   Add the flour, sugar, salt, and vanilla and mix lightly, just enough to incorporate everything.

3   Put the bowl into the food processor, with the kneading hook attached, and start kneading. Add the eggs one at a time. Knead for a few minutes until the batter is nicely uniform.

4   Start adding the butter, a little bit at a time, kneading after each addition. Use a dough scraper to scrape the sides of the bowl and send the batter and the butter back toward the hook. Knead until the batter is very smooth and shiny.

5   Transfer the batter into a buttered or lightly greased bowl, cover with plastic wrap, and let it rise for several hours in a warm spot (3 to 4 hours). The batter should double in volume.

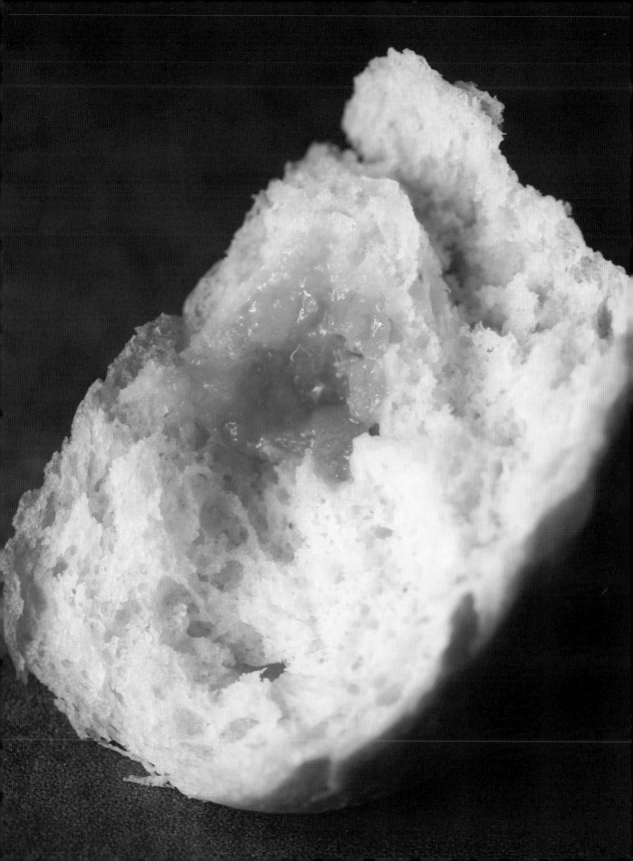

6 Lightly punch down the batter and put it into the refrigerator overnight—this step is essential to facilitate the shaping of the batter.

7 The next day, turn the batter out onto a lightly floured work surface and divide it into small portions using a pastry cutter. For filled mini brioches, I suggest portions of approximately 90 grams.

8 Lightly flatten each piece, put a teaspoon of jam into the hollow, and then close it up again, making a seam to form it into a ball.

9 Place in a buttered tray and let rise for a few hours, depending on the room temperature (usually about 2 hours).

10 Bake in a preheated oven at about 350°F (180°C) for 20 to 25 minutes for mini brioches. If you are making one large brioche, extend the baking time.

VIENNESE PASTRY DOUGH

(FOR CROISSANTS, CHOCOLATE CROISSANTS, AND SWEET RAISIN ROLLS)

Ingredients (for 12 pastries)

130 g of active starter

190 ml of warm milk

40 g of egg yolk

350 g of high-gluten wheat flour

100 g of type T110 or type T150 wheat flour (whole wheat or dark whole wheat)

25 g of softened butter

50 g of powdered sugar

8 g of salt

250 g of butter for flaking (82% fat)

Glaze: 1 egg beaten + 1 tablespoon of water

STEPS

Preparing to soak: Pour all of the ingredients except for the butter for flaking into the bowl of the food processor and knead them until the dough is smooth. Wrap it in plastic wrap and put it into the refrigerator overnight.

In the meantime, roll out the butter for flaking between two sheets of parchment paper to give it a square shape, which will make it easier to integrate it into the dough during the folding phase. Chill the butter.

Folding and rest: The next day, first take out the butter and leave it at room temperature for 20 minutes so that it will have the right texture, will not be too hard, and will be easier to spread. Take the dough out of the refrigerator and spread it into a square. Place the butter in the center, and then close the edges back up like an envelope, enclosing the butter in the center.

On a very lightly floured work surface, spread the dough into a rectangle three times as long as it is wide and make three simple folds in total, letting it stand in the refrigerator for at least 30 minutes between each fold.

After all the folds are done, put the flaked dough back into the refrigerator for at least an hour and a half. This resting time will make the shaping easier.

Shaping and glazing: To make croissants, roll the dough into a 5 mm-thick rectangle and cut it into 10 triangles. Make a small incision at the base of each triangle, stretching it and rolling it to shape croissants without pressing too hard. Give each croissant a first glaze.

To make chocolate croissants, or pains au chocolat, roll the dough out, again to a thickness of 5 mm. Place little sticks of chocolate along the edges; these will serve as markers for cutting out rectangles. Then fold the dough over each little stick of chocolate and place another little stick of chocolate on top, before rolling the dough over onto itself to make a chocolate croissant. Give each chocolate croissant a first egg glaze.

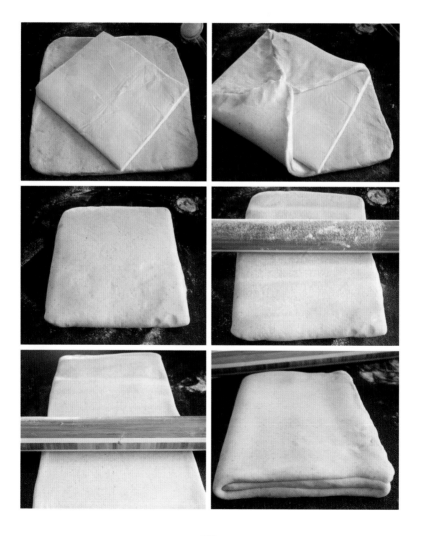

You can also use this dough to make sweet raisin rolls.

Rest: Let the pastries stand for several hours—an average of 4 hours, although it will depend on the room temperature and could take up to 6 hours. The pastries must have risen before you bake them.

Baking: Glaze the pastries a second time before putting them into an oven that has been preheated to about 400°F (200°C). Bake for 10 minutes at 400°F (200°C) and then turn the temperature down to 350°F (180°C) and bake for another 15 minutes. The pastries should be nicely golden when you take them out of the oven.

BASIC MUFFIN RECIPE

Ingredients

180 g of active starter

175 g of water (or half water and half milk)

80 g of powdered sugar

20 g of honey

75 g of melted butter

320 g of type T45 or type T55 flour (pastry or all-purpose)

1 teaspoon of baking powder

1 pinch of salt

1 teaspoon of vanilla extract

Your choice of garnish: red berries, bananas, chocolate chips, etc.

STEPS

1 Pour the water (or water-and-milk mixture) into a bowl, add the starter, and mix to dissolve. Add the flour, mix quickly with a spoon, and let it stand for 1 to 2 hours, depending on the room temperature.

2 Add the melted butter, the sugar, and the honey, and mix. Then incorporate the salt, the baking powder, and the vanilla. Sometimes it will be necessary to beat the batter for a long time, ideally using the flat beater attachment on the food processor, in order to obtain a nicely uniform batter.

3 Add the fruit, chocolate chips, and/or chopped dried fruit, if you are using them.

4 Fill the muffin tins 2/3 full of batter, using a spoon.

5 Preheat the oven to 350°F (180°C). Bake for 20 minutes. The muffins should be golden when you take them out of the oven.

SHORT-CRUST PASTRY BASE

(FOR PIES AND QUICHES)

Ingredients

220 g of type T45 or type T55 flour (pastry or all-purpose)

200 g of very cold butter

2 tablespoons of confectioner's sugar (for sweet doughs)

2 generous pinches of salt

80 to 100 g of active or inactive starter

Glaze: 1 egg yolk + 1 tablespoon of water

STEPS

1   Pour the flour, sugar, and salt into a bowl. Cube the very cold butter and cut it into the dough until you get a crumbed texture. This step can be done with a food processor equipped with a knife blade attachment.

2   Pour in the starter and start pulling the dough together, without kneading. Add the starter just a little at a time until all of the dough can be picked up as a single mass. Cover with plastic wrap and refrigerate for several hours, ideally overnight.

3   The next day, take the dough out of the refrigerator and let it stand for a few minutes at room temperature so that it can soften a little and be easier to work with.

This dough is ideal as the base for a rustic fruit tart; simply spread it out, garnish the center with fruit (for example, fruit compote and peaches), fold the edges toward the center, glaze, and sprinkle with sugar before putting it into the oven for 20 minutes at 400°F (200°C). A culinary delight!

FERMENTED PASTA

Ingredients

100 g of hard wheat flour

200 g of type T55 (all-purpose) flour

80 g of active starter

2 eggs

1 tablespoon of olive oil

1 generous pinch of salt

A little bit of water and flour to adjust the consistency

STEPS

1   Pour the two kinds of flour into a bowl and add the salt, the olive oil, and the active starter. Mix with a wooden spoon.

2   Add the two eggs and start mixing and kneading the dough by hand so that you can collect it into a ball. Depending on the degree of absorption of the flours, it might be necessary to adjust the consistency of the dough with a little bit of water. If, on the other hand, the dough seems too soft, add a little bit of flour to obtain a consistency that is firm but not too dry. You also don't want the dough to be sticky.

3   Roll the dough and cover it with plastic wrap. Put it in the refrigerator for a few hours, ideally overnight.

4   The next day, using a rolling pin, roll the dough out into a ribbon on a floured work surface. Put the dough through the pasta roller a first time, then fold the dough back onto itself and put it through the roller a second time, making sure to flour the roller each time. The third time, use a particular shape, such as the tagliatelle cutter, for example. As you finish cutting the pieces of pasta, lay them out to dry on a pasta drying rack or on a tray covered with a dry, lightly floured cloth.

If you don't have a pasta roller, you can carry out these steps with a rolling pin, using the rolling pin to flatten the pasta folded over on itself. Then cut the strips of tagliatelle with a knife.

Cook the pasta in salted boiling water for a few minutes before draining and then tasting.

WILD YEAST DOUGHNUTS

Ingredients

150 g of active starter

150 ml of warm milk

50 g of powdered sugar

150 g of eggs

70 g of softened butter

450 g of type T55 or T45 (pastry or all-purpose) wheat flour

1 tablespoon of vanilla extract

7 g of salt

STEPS

Preparing the dough: In the bowl of the food processor, dissolve the active starter in the warm milk. Add the eggs, the vanilla, and the sugar, then mix.

Add the flour and the salt and start kneading. Once the dough is uniform, start incorporating the softened butter, continuing to knead the whole time. The dough should be smooth and shiny.

First rise: Transfer the dough to a greased container and cover. Let it stand for 3 to 4 hours at room temperature. After this first resting period, lightly punch down the dough with the palm of your hand. Cover and put into the refrigerator overnight.

Division and cutting out: Turn the dough out onto a floured work surface and, using a pastry roller, flatten it to a thickness of 1.5 cm. Using a cookie cutter or a cup, cut out the doughnuts. As you cut them out, place them on a plate covered in floured parchment paper.

Second rise: Let the doughnuts stand for 2 to 2 1/2 hours at room temperature. They should double in volume.

Frying: Heat oil in a pot or preheat the fryer. Submerge the doughnuts in the hot oil, monitoring them as they fry. As soon as they start rising back to the surface, turn them over and fry them until they are golden brown. Drain each one, as it is finished, on a wire rack.

Glaze: You can glaze the doughnuts with powdered sugar, melted chocolate, or cinnamon sugar.

Eat them while they are still warm, if possible!

PIZZA DOUGH

Ingredients

150 g of active starter

320 g of water

500 g of pizza flour (or if that's not available, all-purpose wheat flour)

10 g of salt

10 g of olive oil, and some more to use along the way

STEPS

Autolysis: Pour the water, the flour, and the olive oil into a large bowl. Mix briefly with a wooden spoon to thoroughly combine. Let stand for a 30- to 45-minute autolysis.

Adding the starter: Add the starter by mixing it into the dough using a wooden spoon or a food processor with a dough hook. Knead until the starter is completely incorporated. Cover with a cloth and let stand for another 20 minutes.

Incorporating the salt: Add the salt and knead until it is well integrated into the dough and the dough is nice and smooth.

First rest: Transfer the dough into a greased container, cover, and let stand at room temperature for 3 to 4 hours.

Dividing and pre-shaping: Turn the dough out onto a floured work surface. Divide the dough into 4 or 5 sections, depending on how big you want them to be, using the pastry cutter. Pre-shape, rolling each section.

Second rest, in the refrigerator: Oil your hands and pick up each ball, one at a time, lightly coating it in olive oil. Place each ball on a plate, cover it with plastic wrap, and put it into the refrigerator at least overnight. The dough can rest in the refrigerator for as much as 24 to 48 hours.

Shaping, garnishing, and baking: When you are ready to make the pizza, take the dough out of the refrigerator, flour it, and roll it out. Garnish to taste (with tomato sauce and mozzarella for the simplest kind of pizza, a pizza margherita), and bake it at 480°F (250°C) for 15 minutes.

WHOLE-WHEAT ENGLISH MUFFINS

Ingredients

200 g of active starter

150 g of type T150 (dark) whole-wheat flour (preferably stone-ground)

330 g of type T55 or type T65 white flour (all-purpose or high-gluten)

140 ml of warm milk

140 g of water

30 g of softened butter

9 g of salt

STEPS

1   Into a bowl, pour first the milk and the water and then the active starter, which should float on top of the liquid.

2   Add the two kinds of flour, mix with a wooden spoon, and let stand for 30 minutes.

3   Add the salt and the butter and knead for several minutes using the food processor until the batter is smooth and starts to detach from the sides of the bowl.

4   Cover the bowl with plastic wrap and let stand for 3 to 4 hours, depending on the room temperature. The batter should double in volume. Put it in the refrigerator to slow it down overnight.

5   Take out the batter and divide it into several portions, each the size of a tangerine; roll them and then let them stand for 1 to 2 hours on a cloth sprinkled with a flour-semolina mixture.

6   Bake in a hot, ungreased pan. The English muffins should be nicely browned on each side.

Eat these lightly toasted with butter and jam. A delight!

RED PESTO AND PARMESAN ROLLS

Ingredients

100 g of active starter

500 g of type T45 flour (pastry)

150 g of warm reduced-fat milk

150 g of water at room temperature

65 g of softened butter

8 g of salt

40 g of parmesan

3 tablespoons of red pesto

Glaze: 1 egg yolk + 1 tablespoon of water

Seeds (I used yellow flaxseed)

Chopped parsley or basil

STEPS

1 Pour the milk, water, and active starter into the bowl; mix and dissolve with a wooden spoon, and then add the flour. Mix for a few seconds without kneading. Let stand for 40 minutes.

2 Put the bowl into the food processor, add the salt and the softened butter, and knead until the dough comes away from the sides of the bowl. It should be very smooth and uniform.

3 Roll the dough and let it stand in an oiled bowl for 3 to 4 hours, depending on the room temperature. The dough should at least double in volume.

4 Turn the dough out onto a floured surface and spread it out into a rectangle using a rolling pin, until it is 1 cm thick.

5 With a spatula, spread the pesto over the whole surface of the dough, and then sprinkle with parmesan and chopped parsley. Roll it up tightly into a sausage shape and put it into the refrigerator to chill for 30 minutes to facilitate cutting.

6 Cut into 1.5 cm long sections, using a wet knife, and place on a baking sheet covered with parchment paper, or into a greased baking pan.

7 Let stand for 2 to 2 1/2 hours, glaze, and sprinkle the flaxseed on top.

8 Put into the oven and bake at 375°F (190°C) for about 20 minutes. The rolls should be nicely golden.

When you take them out of the oven, you can pour a light drizzle of olive oil over the rolls. Before serving, sprinkle each roll with chopped fresh or dried parsley.

TROUBLESHOOTING: PROBLEMS AND SOLUTIONS

WHAT SHOULD I DO IF MY STARTER...

...IS STILL COMPLETELY SOFT AND HASN'T REALLY STARTED TO BUBBLE, EVEN AFTER A FEW DAYS?

Sometimes a starter will grow more slowly than usual; it seems tired and doesn't produce many bubbles. This could be the result of a multitude of factors, such as the quality of the flour used to maintain it. Before deciding to throw out the starter, or to begin a new one, you can try to "revive it." Here are a few ways to do that:

- If you have been feeding your starter only white flour, try refreshing it using organic rye flour, ideally type T150 or T170. Add a few drops of honey.
- For a small portion of the water that you use to refresh the starter, substitute fermented fruit water (see page 42).
- If the temperature is cool, try putting the starter in a warm place after you have refreshed it.

...PRODUCES AN UNPLEASANT SMELL OR BECOMES MOLDY?

Over the days, weeks, and months of using a starter, you end up developing the ability to detect the health of the starter by its smell alone. The way it smells when it is healthy is often similar to the smell of yogurt. It is a pleasant, agreeable, milky, and almost fruity smell. But it can happen that one's starter starts to give off a very disagreeable odor!

A starter that smells bad or, worse, has developed moldy spots will end up in the garbage; it is important not to take a risk, so this is a time to establish a new starter and to make sure to take very good care of it this time around!

...DEVELOPS A CRUST ON THE SURFACE?

When you are first developing your starter, it is stored in a jar, and you need to cover the jar, not leave it open. You don't have to go as far as sealing the jar. You just need to put a lid or a small saucer on top of it to protect it and keep it from developing a crust.

If, however, a crust does form, all you have to do is to integrate it into the starter the next time you refresh it, starting by dissolving it in the water that you use to feed the starter. Do not forget to cover your container.

...HAS SEPARATED INTO TWO PARTS?

When a starter is stored in the refrigerator for a longish time, you will sometimes observe a separation in the jar, with dough on the bottom and water, sometimes dark-colored, on top. This most often happens when the starter has been stored for too long without being fed.

There is no need to throw away the water that is floating on top; all you have to do is mix the whole thing together in the jar with a spoon and then quickly refresh the starter!

WHAT SHOULD I DO IF MY DOUGH...

...DOESN'T RISE?

During the fermentation stages, it can happen that you will be disappointed because you don't see many signs of the fermentation you are looking for. This can result, most often, from a starter that is too sluggish or room temperatures that are too low.

- Always make sure that your starter is active enough when you are using it to make bread. It is important to be patient and not to use a starter in the first days of its development, even if it seems to be very active. A wild yeast starter is the product of a balance of microorganisms, and that balance cannot be attained until several days have gone by. Thus, it is essential to respect this process.

- Before starting to make bread dough, check the state of your starter by testing it. The flotation test explained on page 40 will allow you to make sure that it is active enough and ready to form the basis of bread dough.

- During the winter, room temperatures can be very low, which will slow down the fermentation of your starter. To address this issue, put your dough in a warm place, for instance near a radiator.

- The rising times shown in the recipes are merely meant as a guide. The best way to produce successful wild yeast bread is to respect the time it needs for rising. This time is unique to each starter, even if we can indicate rough averages. If it seems as though the dough is not rising enough, it is better to prolong the rising stages than to rush things and be disappointed in the end.

...IS TOO SOFT AND STICKY?

A dough that is too soft and too wet is often hard to handle, especially when you are just starting out.

- Never pour in all the water at once right from the start, especially if you have not yet mastered the handling of your flour and haven't learned all its qualities. There is no point in overhydrating a dough if you are then going to end up with a mass that is impossible to shape. It is important to start gradually and to hydrate the dough a little bit at a time so that you can adjust the quantity of water as needed as you go along. In this way, you can obtain a dough that you can easily work with.

- Try to salvage the dough by adding in extra folds. This might help a little in giving the dough more stability.

- Use a pastry cutter to handle the dough, and avoid, as far as possible, adding too much flour while you are shaping the dough.

- Before you put the dough in the oven, after letting it rise at room temperature, put the pan into the fridge for a few minutes so that you can then score the loaf more easily and the dough will not sag too much during baking.

WHAT SHOULD I DO IF MY BREAD...

...IS TOO DENSE?

When you take the bread out of the oven, it looks good, but when you slice it, you find that the crumb is too dense and heavy. This could be the result of a starter that was not active enough, a dough that wasn't hydrated enough, or not enough rising time.

- Was the starter active enough? Did it pass the flotation test?
- Hydrate the dough more thoroughly the next time, but go gently; you don't have to flood your flour to get an airy crumb.
- Respect the rising times. As noted above, every starter is unique and has its own rising speed!

...IS TOO ACIDIC?

The bread is pretty to look at, but when you taste it, it's very acidic. This has to do with a starter that was too acidic, which could be due to storage in the fridge or to the use of a firm starter, which can lead to the development of too much acetic acid.

- Use a liquid starter, in other words, one that is hydrated with equal proportions of flour and water. Using a firm starter, when you thought you were using a liquid starter, could sometimes come from having fed the starter using volumes rather than weights. It is important to always weigh your ingredients to make sure you keep the proportions the way they should be.
- Use a starter that you refreshed several hours before making the dough, and then store it in a warm spot and not in the refrigerator.

...PRODUCES A STICKY AND UNDERCOOKED CRUMB?

When you cut it open, the bread leaves traces of dough on the knife and the crumb is sticky or seems undercooked.

- Respect the necessary rising and baking times. Personally, I prefer a well-browned bread to one that is undercooked, with a pale crust and a doughy, sticky crumb, which is unpleasant to eat, especially if it contains a lot of rye.
- Let the bread cool and stand after baking; don't slice into it right after you take it out of the oven.

HAPPY BAKING, MY FRIENDS!

At the beginning, the idea of creating your own liquid wild yeast starter, maintaining it, and using it to make your own bread can seem mystifying, especially if you start with the idea that wild yeast starter is complicated and hard to manage! Believe me when I tell you that sometimes all it takes is trying again to completely change how things look—one fresh start to become completely adept at making and using starter and all the multitude of options that it opens up to us. From bread to brioche, by way of croissants and cakes, almost anything you bake can lend itself to this kind of leavening, providing greater tasting pleasure and more personal satisfaction. . . .

A starter can last for years, can be a precious ingredient in your daily life, and can even be passed on and shared. You will see that over the course of your attempts and the many slices of bread that you get to eat warm, a very simple but wonderful thing starts to happen: you start to take pleasure again in making, with your own hands, something as grand as your daily bread!

ACKNOWLEDGMENTS

Bread means sharing, and what would sharing be without gratitude?

This book has been, above all, the product of collaboration, and therefore, my thanks go first of all to my editor and to the whole team at Eyrolles, who once again trusted me and followed me on this great adventure.

A very big thank-you to Marie-Béatrice Queinnec and to Le Creuset for their fantastic pots.

Huge thanks to my virtual and real-life breadmaking friends, who never stopped encouraging me, especially my friend Valérie, aka Coc' La Cairote, who is every bit as addicted to wild yeast starter as I am.

All of the recipes in this book, as well as the ones that I have shared on my blog or on social media, were tested and produced by me personally. But I must also thank my team of tester/guinea pigs, my loved ones, who played along and became true culinary critics in the process!

Many thanks to my parents.

And to Sofia, the love of my life.